GOING TO
WAIT!

G-6198

# GOING TO WAIT!

## AFRICAN AMERICAN CHURCH WORSHIP RESOURCES BETWEEN PENTECOST AND ADVENT

James Abbington
and Linda H. Hollies

GIA Publications, Inc.
Chicago • www.giamusic.com

G-6198
Copyright © 2003
GIA Publications, Inc.
7404 S. Mason Ave., Chicago, IL 60638

www.giamusic.com

ISBN: 1-57999-262-5
Book layout and design: Robert Sacha

"Let the Word of God dwell in you richly in all wisdom,
teaching and admonishing one another in psalms and hymns and spiritual songs,
singing with grace in your hearts to the Lord!"

—Colossians 3: 16 NIV

# TABLE OF CONTENTS

# DEDICATIONS AND ACKNOWLEDGEMENTS

This work is dedicated to every church musician, choir director, choir, singing group, and soloist who I have met and worked with over the years.

As a child, I remember the dedication of Molly Walker and Sally Clark. They "plunked" the old piano at the 17th Street Church of God in Christ where I was raised, and helped me to remember and come to love the old songs of the Church. As a young adult, I remember John Berry and Matthew Whittington, who gave us the sounds that assisted the choir in rendering anthems in grand style. As a pastor in training, I am appreciative of my mentor, Dr. Willie B. Clay, who had every choir: the Chancel, the Gospel, the Young Adult, the Inspirational, and the Youth choirs, sing every Sunday. He taught me how to richly feed every member of the congregation in song. That way, no one would have an excuse to stay home until his or her "favorite" choir sang! It's a lesson I yet value today.

As a United Methodist pastor, I have had the opportunity to work with some of the best in the music industry. I give God thanks for my first Minister of music, Diane Mitchell. Diane and the members of Praise fed my spirit every Sunday in a primarily Anglo congregation. The anointing of the Holy Spirit rests heavily and mightily upon this woman, and I thank God for putting her in my life. Linda Elliott, at my second charge, is another lover of music who can translate it beyond the page. Bobby Battle helped me to move my Black congregation to the new innovation called the keyboard! And every Sunday, we sang *Speak to My Heart* before I preached. It was an awesome experience that brought deliverance to many souls. Thank you to Cynthia Wilson-Felder, Johnnetta Page, Jannette Chandler-Kotey and The Anointed Jackson Singers, along with my son, concert flautist Grelon Renard Everett, my brother, concert violinist Obed Shelton, and my daughters, Grian Hollies and Vera Riley, for always blessing me with their ministry of music.

I am not sure where the idea originated that sparked my interest in writing liturgies. However, I am sure that it was a gift from God to encourage the saints. It was from this writing venture that Dr. Melva Costen took note and made use of my work in her classes at The Interdenominational Theological Center. She introduced it to Dr. James Abbington, who called and asked if I would teach a class at Hampton. He and co-director, Royzell Dilliard allowed me a rare privilege, as both a female pastor and a non-Baptist, to interact with musicians from across the nation. This work is a direct result. My prayer is that it will assist musicians and choirs to better minister in their God given role of spreading the Living Word through song.

Because of my work at The Hampton Musician's Guild Workshop, I have been blessed to take some time and work with an awesome Baptist pastor, Derrick Lewis-Noble and Minister of Music, Lamar James and praise Leader, George Lowe Celeste Babers, RayAnn Booker and Brian Lowe; Directors, Jean Pittman, Kim Jarnejan and Billy Davis at the New Hope Baptist Church in Grand Rapids, Michigan. With you, I'm on the journey, Going to Wait! And, on this journey, we all need a song! Sing a prayer for me, as I sing one for you along the way. Shalom, my friend, God's best Shalom!

—Sista Linda H. Hollies

# DEDICATIONS AND ACKNOWLEDGEMENTS

This work is dedicated in loving memory of two of the greatest pastors, worship leaders, brothers, friends and confidants that God ever blessed me to know who departed this life within two months of each other last year – *The Reverend Dr. Nathaniel Tyler-Lloyd*, Pastor of the Trinity Baptist Church in Bronx, New York for 42 years whose passed away on May 29, 2002; and *The Reverend Dr. Dwight M. Jackson*, Pastor of the Amity Baptist Church in Jamaica, New York for 16 years who passed away on July 23, 2002. I had the distinct privilege of planning, conducting, and evaluating worship with these men of God and their wonderful and loving congregations respectively for many years. Their love for God, The Church, God's people, music and worship will always be remembered and will live on.

I received an anonymous email over a year ago that read, "I believe that friends are quiet angels who lift us to our feet when our wings have trouble remembering how to fly." While I have been unable to find the author of these profound words, I have borrowed them to express my sincere gratitude and appreciation for the "quiet angels" who have prayed, encouraged, telephoned, emailed, stopped by for a quick visit, and supported me during this endeavor.

I gratefully acknowledge the unswerving love and prayers of my mother, Daisy Ann Barlow; the support and encouragement of my Shaw University administrators, colleagues, and Visual and Performing Arts faculty: Dr. Ernest L. Pickens, Dr. Lillie M. Boyd, Mr. Charles Tita, Dr. Bradley Hunnicutt, Ms. Loñieta Cornwall, Mr. George Hatcher, Mrs. Nikita Shah-Pace, Mrs. Julya Oberg, Mrs. Minnie McMillan, Mr. Kenneth Hinton, and Mrs. Beena Ollapally; my competent and reliable secretary, Mrs. Mildred Hooker, and my faithful and meticulous student administrative assistant, Antwan Lofton.

There are those friends of many years whose voices on the other end of the telephone, humorous and uplifting messages and emails have provided me with more support than they will ever know: Alfred Bolden, Jr., Erin C. Smith, Arron Brown, Angelo Henderson, Ted and Pamela Jones, Dr. Gale Isaacs, Drs. Calvin and Uzee Brown, Jr., Reverend Lisa Weaver, Charles B. Jones, and others too numerous to mention.

Don Walston, President and CEO of Howard Perry and Walston Realtors of Raleigh, NC continues to be a true model example of generosity, kindness, patience, concern, and understanding of my professional and musical efforts, specifically with The Shaw University Choir—he has been God-sent.

I have incurred a tremendous debt of gratitude during the writing of this book from my GIA family: Ed Harris, Alec Harris, Bob Batastini, Robert Sacha, Jeff Mickus, Vicki Krstansky, Laura Cacciottilo, and all the rest, for your kindness, support, competence, and efficiency. Without all of you, this would not be a reality.

What can I say about Sista Linda? She has truly become my sista, friend, counselor, advisors, colleague, and second-time, co-author. I thank God for allowing this partnership for the people of God.

Language fails to express my heartfelt appreciation to all of you who have "lifted me to my feet" on those many occasions when I had "trouble remembering how to fly."

—James Abbington

# INTRODUCTION

God is! The blanks can be filled in with so many various and descriptive adjectives. Any one that we use fails to adequately encompass the length, breath and depth of who and what God really is in this world and beyond.

Writing this in the fall season, on a color tour through the eastern portion of our nation, I can tell you that God is an artist of indescribable comprehension! Looking at groves of trees nestled upon The Allegheny Mountains, the scene takes away my breath. The sky is azure blue; the clouds are fluffy and white. The fields are golden. The cooling water meanders here and there; streams, rivers, creeks and lakes. But, upon the hills sit a collective of colors painted every color imaginable. God is artist extraordinaire!

Who told which trees to turn a sparkling orange, dazzling red, brilliant yellow, hazy shades of purple or evergreen? Who whispered "change" to the season and sent a nip into the air; falling leaves to the ground; told flowers to fade but chrysanthemums to bud? Who orchestrated the winds to shift; told warm weather to fade and called colder air to be summoned from the north water reservoirs? What producer told fruit, grain and potatoes to yield their crop? What force dispatched little birds to begin their flight south? Who speaks to caterpillars the time to begin their metamorphosis process of spinning cocoons? Who tells earth to shut down production and to prepare for winter rest? What power forces fish to sink lower into undisturbed waters while bears begin to feel and to experience their slumber throughout another season? As the leaves fall, not one looks like another. The snowflakes are being prepared, one by one, each one already accounted for and named! What makes these mountains stand, yielding coal generation after generation, warming a world that knew nothing of fire when Adam and Eve were created? How is it that clouds above keep oceans and rivers afloat, and trees provide both air and protection from the sun?

All of Mother Nature's magnificence calls forth our hymns of praise and worship. "Great is Thy Faithfulness" surely testifies to God's artistry without painter, landscape artist or production crew! "Our God Is An Awesome God," merely whispers at the awesomeness of The Creator.

For no one word can ever contain our adoration of God. There is not any single human element of speech to provide expression of all God is! Therefore, we simply worship God in singing hymns. Hymns magnify God. Hymns declare our worship of The Ancient of Days. Hymns address our need to say something about our adoration of The One Who Was, The One Who Is and The One Who Is To Come! Hymns concentrate our attention on The First and The Last. Hymns utter our unspeakable thanks to The Giver of All!

A hymn takes our focus from us. A hymn's focus is The Great I Am, who though available to us, is far beyond us, even above and beneath us. A hymn removes our train of thought from our immediate condition, circumstances and situations to point us toward our help, our protection, our refuge and our shelter. A hymn moves us to look up! A hymn pulls us to magnify The Sovereign God who is yet in control of the whole wide world. All is well with a hymn for our God reigns!

Hymns call us to true worship. Hymns help us to see God's vast glory. Hymns help us to remember what God has already done. We join with the angelic forces to bow down in reverence before God's Throne as we worship with a hymn. Hymns assist us in believing that what God has done already, down through the ages, God will "encore!" God will do it again, in our time, the hymn assures us as they anchor our faith in The Mystery.

The God of every season is faithful. The God of winter's frozen, sleeping beauty does it again, year after year. That's faithfulness. The God of overcast days and cloudy skies is the same God who speaks buds into sprouting and glaciers begin to float in the spring. That's faithfulness. The God of warming air is the same God who commands the sun to become butter yellow and the birds to migrate back to sing for us again in the summer heat. That's faithfulness. And, it's this same

God who prepares an abundant harvest for the world's nourishment in the fall. That's faithfulness. Hymns attempt to capture God's faithful wonders and set them to music for us to express our thanks and appreciation.

As the Church "goes into all the world" we need marching music. We need the melody that ties us with the faithful who went before us. Our children, grandchildren and great-grandchildren, for as many generations as the Lord allows to follow us, need to know the tunes of our faith in God. So, we place special emphasis on hymns and anthems in both volumes of *Waiting to Go*, and now, *Going to Wait*.

Kirk Franklin, Yolanda Adams, Mary and John P. Kee utilize the messages of ancient tunes! They have updated the tempo, contemporized the melody and added new beats, but they continue to depend upon the sacred words of The Church's great hymns and anthems. These "new artists" are not original. For the deeds, acts, movements, miracles and signs of God have been noted and penned down through the years.

Ecclesiastes 1:9, reminds us, "There is nothing new under the sun."

There is a difference between hymns, anthems, gospel and contemporary music. We need to teach our young people the full range of our faith. It's wonderful to have the "boomers" coming back to The Church. It's awesome to have our youth "fishing for religion." Plus, we only exist due to the thrill of having our elders remain in our pews as anchors to our past. Each one of these groups need to be musically fed and challenged to grow in our faith journey. Teaching, singing and utilizing the hymns and anthems allow for inter-generational worship. Watch the faces of the congregation as a soloist sings a metered hymn and then the Praise Team or choir swings into the rhythm that is popular today. We are all on the journey together! This army needs to march to a coordinated beat. Let's keep singing til the power of The Lord comes down to dwell among us, tabernacle within us and remains within us as we Go to Wait!

# ABOUT THE CHRISTIAN YEAR

Pentecost is the occasion of the sending down from heaven, the inner dwelling God who takes up abode in us, walks beside us, goes before us and teaches us the lessons of living for Jesus Christ in the world. The Holy Spirit dances into this room of waiting and praying people to touch them, empower them, embolden them and dispatch them unto the uttermost corner of the world to proclaim the mystery we call Jesus Christ. Pentecost is the sending forth of a group of scared, timid, and hidden folks from their closed Upper Room into the entire world. Pentecost is the sending out of men and women to testify to the change, the difference and the transformation that the power of The Holy Spirit has made in them.

The season of Pentecost comes with a message to these who had been tarrying, waiting, praying and discussing the post-Resurrection events concerning Jesus. The new message is "Get ready! Set! Go!" The waiting time has passed. The Comforter has come. It is

time to put the new mandate of Jesus into practice. We now call that mandate The Great Commission. Jesus gave it to The Church of God on the day of Ascension. "All authority in heaven and on earth has been given unto me. Go out and train everyone you meet in the world. Go far and near teaching them this way of life. Mark them by baptism in the name of The Creator, Son and Holy Spirit. Then, instruct them in the practice of all I have commanded you. I'll be with you as you do this, day after day up to the end of the age." (Matthew 28:18-20; from *The Message Bible*; Peterson, Eugene; NavPress, 2002)

The Church is now ready to go. The Church has been given its purpose, its mission, its charge, its mandate and its support. Our purpose is to go and to reach the whole wide world, telling them that Jesus Christ now lives so that we may live eternally. Our mission is to reach them and to teach them about a new way of thinking and behaving. The charge given to the whole Church is to baptize new believers and mark them by the name of their new "owners." After baptism, we are to indoctrinate them into the faith. We can do our jobs because of the support of The One in whose name we are given power and authority to go and just do it!

Think about it! We are the people on the move for Jesus. We are the feet, the hands, the mouth, the arms, and the legs that carry the message of life to a world that is dying. Our purpose is not to be so concerned with the personalities that we encounter in our local worship spaces. Our purpose is not to be so hung up on our particular pastor until no one else can teach us life lessons. Our purpose is not to be so overly concerned with the maintenance of bricks and mortar until we forget that we are called to be Church on the go!

Our mission is to get souls as our efforts and not to simply focus all of energies on our local church activities. Yes! We do need tithers and givers. Yes! We do need the funds to finance the ministries. Yes! We need to keep the lights, gas, staff salaries and pastors package up to date. But, our total budget should not be fixed in house. For outreach is our aim. Reaching new converts is our game! They are not simply to come and see the beautiful edifices that we have built to soothe our egos about the ancestors who labored long ago. Instead, we are to go and reach them because we have a message from the Savior for them.

Our charge is to baptize new believers into the faith and to celebrate their coming into the family of God. As they are marked with a watery grave, the angels are celebrating. As they are marked and branded as those who have a new beginning, the angels are doing the holy dance. As the are taken down into the death of Jesus and raised to new life in him, the angels are writing names down in glory as the noise goes forth with joy. So, surely we celebrate with the angels and market for the world to see that "they" have lost souls that we found along our way. These new lives will market for us. These new converts are our best advertisement. These new inductees are walking, talking and living testimonies to the power of that marvelous name, Jesus Christ.

It is our character that teaches new converts how they are to live. It is not our winning personalities that impress them. It is not our seniority in the local building that helps them to change their life styles. It is not the whoop of the preacher or the melodious harmony of the singing groups that will keep them in this new way. It is the character that they see reflected in us, day by day and week after week.

It is our value system, in the Church of the Living God, which says people are important. It is the norm that we evidence to people that we care about them in the manner that Jesus cares for us all. Our character, rooted in the personality of only Jesus Christ, none other, makes us soul winners and people keepers! For the power of The Holy Spirit has come to keep us and to make us excellent role models for the whole, wide world to witness.

Pentecost leads us into Trinity Sunday where we celebrate the Triune God. Following this acknowledgment of Creator, Son and Holy Spirit we move into what is called Ordinary Time. This is a season marked by the color green, that represents our growth without benefit of celebrations and festivities. This is the longest season of The Christian Year. We are sustained by God's Word, God's people in community and by the power of prayer and The Holy Spirit. This season is a daily walk with God as we live out our confessions of faith in the world. In the mundane duties of life, we are to be faith-filled witnesses, Going to Wait!

Our waiting is not one of laziness and complacency. Our waiting is not one of anxiousness and fretfulness. Our waiting is not a time of sloth and doing nothing. We wait as soldiers. We have been given an assignment. It is to go and to make disciples. Wherever we go, whatever we do, whenever the opportunity arises we are to be at our duty of finding and making disciples. We have not been left alone. We have not been forsaken. We have not been abandoned. We have the whole Trinity as our cheerleaders, intercessors and divine intervention. Yet, the task of going to make things happens is with us. The ball is in our court. Our time of sitting, pondering, pontificating and reflecting is over! It's time to look out at the fields, ripe for harvest and to notice that there are too few laborers and the time is short. We are to pray that God send others to help with the assignment. But, if they don't ever arrive, this duty post is ours! Our job, as Priests and Levites, is to make it happen!

"On the seventh day God rested from all the creative labor. God blessed the seventh day and made it a Holy Day." Genesis 2:2 details how God ceased work and left it up to those in The Garden to take control of and maintain it in good order. God sat down in order that we might go to work. The fanfare of Creation was complete. It was beautiful, awesome, wonderful and very good. Everything had been given reproductive powers. Seed time and harvest, a natural food chain was established and both animals and mammals were given the ability to mate and keep creation going. It was all good. And, it was left to The Original Parents.

The spectacular, the phenomenal and the downright preposterous had been achieved. All that was required was maintenance. It had been a birthday gift prepared for the first human beings. God had insured that all they would ever need had been supplied. It should have been an easy task to fulfill. But, the story does not end with a "happily ever after" note. Before we get to Chapter Four, the Fall has taken place. Innocence is dead. The Original Parents have played the parts of designers and gone to hide behind bushes, praying not to be discovered. Then God comes inquiring, "Adam, where are you?"

Of course, we know that God was not ignorant of their deeds or their hiding place. The question comes to each of us, Adam, that we are today. For Adam is a dirt being. Adam is a weak vessel. Adam has issues. He always had and always will! For Adam was created a little lower than the angels and given both intellect and free will. So, the question, "Adam, where are you?" comes to ask Adam to think about where the rupture in this holy and human relationship lies. For God left them on their own honor during the day. God only came to walk and talk with them in the cool of the evening, after their assigned tasks were complete. However, when God came for an accounting of their day, they failed to appear. They had gone to wait for the benediction!

In the New Testament account of this same story or metaphor, we know that as soon as Jesus was buried in a borrowed tomb, with most of his crew in hiding, missing the funeral and the burial, the boys returned to fishing. They forgot their last assignment. They walked away from their post of duty. And, it was on the river bank that Jesus found them and called to them with a new question. "Children, do you have any fish?" They had been assigned the role of fishers of souls. They had been told to work while it was day. They had been told to take what they knew into the world. And, Jesus caught them hiding behind fishing gear and empty nets!

Jesus sent them back to Jerusalem into hiding until the Holy Spirit was dispatched. The story is told of the day that Jesus returned to heaven and was greeted by the angelic host. "Did you leave them with a campaign strategy?" asked one. The answer was "No." Well, did you leave instructions for a worldwide media blitz?" asked another. "No." Well, thye don't have computers, newspapers and televisions, how will your three year ministry spread?" asked yet another angel. And, Jesus answered, "I left them my name!"

In this Ordinary Season we have the power and authority his matchless, marvelous and miraculous name. We can call upon this name and growth will occur. We can pray in this name and transformation happens. We can use the name and identify ourselves as his disciples. We can go in his name. We can work in his name. We can heal, set free, teach, preach and encourage in his name. For this is the name that is above every name. This is the name that will cause every knee to bow and every tongue to confess. This is the name at which demons tremble and saints rejoice. For there is yet wonder working power in this name!

We enter Ordinary Season at the mid-point of Spring where nature is just budding and sprouting. This ordinary season takes us through the full bloom of Summer and into the harvest of Fall's crops. There is no limit to the many ways that altars may be dressed to signify the growth in our lives. This is an excellent time to have families bring gifts from their gardens to share.

For the Reproducing God is at it again, renewing and replenishing the earth. We can see our transformation. In this ordinary season, God is checking our fruitfulness or fruitlessness!

Jesus went on a walking expedition one day. Peterson puts it like this: "Then Jesus made a circuit of all the towns and villages. He taught in their meeting, reported kingdom news and healed their diseased bodies, healed their bruised and hurt lives. When he looked out over the crowds, his heart broke. So confused and aimless were the people, like sheep with no shepherd. 'What a huge harvest!' he said to his disciples. 'How few workers! On your knees and pray for harvest hands!' The prayer was no sooner prayed than it was answered. Jesus called twelve of his followers and sent them into the ripe fields. He gave them power to kick out the evil spirits and to care for the bruised and hurt lives. This is the list of those he sent. (Here add your name!) Jesus sent the harvest hands out with this charge: 'Don't begin by traveling to some far-off place to convert unbelievers. And don't try to be dramatic by tackling some public enemy. Go to the lost, confused people right here in the neighborhood. Tell them that the kingdom is here. Bring health to the sick. Raise the dead. Touch the untouchables. Kick out the demons. You have been treated generously, so live generously. Don't think you have to put on a fund-raising campaign before you start. You don't need a lot of equipment. You are the equipment!'" (Matthew 9:35-10:8)

This is the message of *Going to Wait*! We are sent into the world in which we live. We are to be the living Word to those we interact with on a daily basis. The stories of those who struggled to grow and become all they could will encourage and instruct us in the days to come. The songs of Zion will stick in our heads and carry us through the weeks ahead. The prayers of the faithful will utter the words that we cannot find in our times of need. And, the community of the saints will help us to try and to try again. For each of us has the same assignment and that is to be faithful as we *Go to Wait*.

# A WORD ABOUT
# THE REVISED COMMON LECTIONARY

The Revised Common Lectionary was created in 1992 so that there would be a collection of readings from scriptures that could be read in Churches across the world each Sunday, thereby connecting Christians, regardless of denominations. Since the early fourth century, there have been special days, seasons, and festivals that used the same passages or lections. It is from this source that the Common Lectionary made its way from the Catholic Church to other mainline denominations. Use of a Lectionary is not a "standard" pattern in most Black congregations, although many denominations provide them as part of their Christian Year.

The "appeal" of a Lectionary is that it allows congregations to hear parts of the Bible that they would not read on their own. The Holy Scriptures were intended to be read aloud to audiences. Reading in the worship service is a great aid, a necessary consolation, and a method of getting congregations to move past their favorite passages, which make up their personal "canon" of scripture. If your congregation is one that does not make use of a regular calendar of passages to be read during the worship service, there are several ways that other scriptures might be included. The deacons, who begin many worships, could be asked to help the choir by using the passage that the Anthem will uplift. A member of the choir could read a particular passage just before the choir sings to provide the context for the words and music that will follow.

There are multitudes of needs that sit in our pews, and what has led us to preach and sing does not necessarily touch all the hurts, pains, and wounds. However, when we make it a habit to read an Old Testament lesson followed by the Psalm, it can work its healing mystery without the follow-up sermon of explanation. People need to know that the God of "old" is alive, well, and operating in our "today"! The Lectionary ties the Old Testament "testimony" to the Psalm for us. The Old Testament passage should be read first. Then the Lectionary provides for us the "thoughts of reflection" through the Psalms that the later Church remembered and rehearsed about the "former" acts of God on the nation's behalf. We are those who now need to hear the "old" stories and to remember that God continues to act on our behalf!

Another "appeal" of the Lectionary is that it allows continuous portions of scripture to be heard, read, and expounded upon over a course of three years. Year A of The Revised Common Lectionary focuses on the book of Matthew. It also provides for us the stories of the Patriarchs, Matriarchs, and Moses the Law Giver. Year B uses the book of Mark as its Gospel. King David and the historical books are its focus. John is used around Christmas and Easter in Year B. Year C takes us through the book of Luke and tells the ministry of both Elijah and Elisha. During the Easter Season, we are taken through the Acts of The Apostles, which replaces the Old Testament lessons. Psalms are used throughout all

three years to give reflection upon the Hebrew scripture and should be read in this manner.

As a preacher of color, this "rigid" structure didn't "sit" well with me when I first heard of it in seminary. I fought it, because I felt that it didn't allow me freedom in The Holy Spirit. But I forced myself to try it. I pushed myself to see whether or not God "could" speak to me. And I came to discover that my life was made richer, fuller, and more inclusive by its use. It pushed me to "hear" God speak to me! It was out of my spiritual growth that I begin to preach, to call congregations to worship, and to work with musicians to bless those in the pew.

With four scriptures each week to read, digest, and study, there was more than I could possibly use on a Sunday morning. Therefore, our Bible Studies and Sunday Schools were enriched. And I could do sermon prep with pastors in my area who were using the same scriptures. It became a necessary tool for me to "see" what God had to say to me about me!

Therefore, I offer this "gift" to you as a spiritual growth aid. Try it. You'll like it!

# A WORD ABOUT THE MUSICAL SELECTIONS

Martin Luther once said that music is a gift of God "instilled and implanted in all creatures...from the beginning of the world. Nothing is without sound or harmony, but the human voice is the most wonderful gift of all. Therefore, next to the Word of God, music deserves the highest praise."

It is in that spirit that I have had the distinct privilege of entering into a harmonious partnership with Reverend Dr. Linda H. Hollies to make this project possible. Dr. Hollies has provided the Scripture lessons, focus, prayers, and visual arts suggestions for each Sunday from Advent through Pentecost. My task has been to provide musical suggestions that will complement, enhance, reinforce, and support the texts and focus of the day.

While my musical suggestions are not intended to be the complete, final, or definitive selections, they are offered to provide a general direction and focus for planning music for the worship service for the various Sundays. The possibilities are endless! Composers are always writing new compositions, and previously written compositions are being uncovered and reprinted.

Because no particular hymnal in the African American church could provide all of the variety and diversity needed for the scope of this project, I have selected the following hymnals for consideration along with their abbreviations throughout this book:

*AAHH   African American Heritage Hymnal* (Chicago: GIA Publications, 2001).

AME    *AMEC Bicentennial Hymnal* (Nashville: The African Methodist Episcopal Church, 1984).

AMEZ  *The African Methodist Episcopal Zion Bicentennial Hymnal* (New York: The African Methodist Episcopal Zion Church, 1996).

LEVS  *Lift Every Voice and Sing II: An African American Hymnal* (New York: The Church Hymnal Corporation, 1993).

LMGM  *Lead Me, Guide Me: The African American Catholic Hymnal* (Chicago: GIA Publications, 1987).

NNBN  *The New National Baptist Hymnal – 21st Century Edition* (Nashville: Triad Publications, 2001).

TFBF  *This Far by Faith* (Minneapolis: Augsburg Fortress, 1999).

YL    *Yes, Lord! Church of God in Christ Hymnal* (Memphis: The Church of God In Christ Publishing Board, 1982).

HG    *Hymns for the Gospels* (Chicago: GIA Publications, 2001).

Other resources for spirituals and organ music that I frequently recommend include the following:

*The Oxford Book of Spirituals.* Edited by Moses Hogan (New York: Oxford University Press, 2002).

*The Anthology of African American Organ Music, Volumes 1-4.* Edited by Dr. Mickey Thomas Terry (St. Louis, MO; Morning Star Music Publishers) [ongoing].

*Songs of Deliverance: Organ Arrangements and Congregational Acts of Worship for the Church Year Based on African American Spirituals.* By William Farley Smith (Nashville: Abingdon Press, 1996).

After considering the scripture lessons and focus for the Sunday, specific themes, emphases, and key words emerged that guided my selection of appropriate hymns, anthems, spirituals, and gospel selections, as well as organ music. I am certainly aware of the various levels of ability and competency among church music personnel and the variety of instruments that exist in African American churches, and have offered a variety of selections that I hope will provide direction for your thinking and selection process.

Noticeably absent from the listings are suggestions for children's choirs, handbells, instrumental ensembles, and praise and worship teams. It is my hope that titles listed will provide adequate ideas and insight for making those selections. I do not claim to be a specialist in those areas, and therefore make no attempt to offer suggestions. However, a project that includes those selections is much needed.

Pastors, music directors, musicians, and worship leaders should invest in a variety of hymnals for their library for a broader use and selection of hymnody for the congregation. The Hymn Society in the United States and Canada provides the most current and reliable resources for church music. I strongly recommend membership in that organization. The toll free number is 1(800) THE HYMN.

While the accessibility of musical resources written by African Americans has been rather limited in the past, there are more musical selections available now than ever. Most of today's current gospel music by recording artists is available in sheet music and can be ordered from local music dealers. I have personally experienced a tremendous amount of cooperation and success with "N" Time Music in Charlotte, NC. They offer gospel sheet music, songbooks, cassettes and CDs, performance soundtracks and much more. Their address is 4913 Albermarie Road, Suite 103, Charlotte, NC 28205. Their email address is info@ntimemusic.com, and the website is www.ntimemusic.com.

I have also enjoyed many years of reliable, dependable, and courteous service with Lois Fyfe Music in Nashville, TN for all of my choral music and organ music needs. Their address is 2814 Blair Blvd, Nashville,

TN 37212. They can also be reached by calling toll free 1(800) 851-9023. Every choir director and musician should establish a consistent and amicable relationship with a music dealer, which brings me to a very critical issue.

I am most obligated to share with the reader that it is illegal to photocopy music! Composers of great music can not and will not benefit from our illegal photocopying and reproduction of their music. The rewards for their work that we so enjoy are never experienced as long as good, God-fearing church choir directors and musicians keep running to the photocopier and illegally reproducing their music. There are very stringent laws that protect these composers, and it is the responsibility of the church Leaders to insure that those laws are not violated. Please be very mindful of this as you select and perform music.

I am indebted to my friend and colleague, Tony McNeill, Director of Music Ministries at the Friendship Missionary Baptist Church in Charlotte, NC, for allowing me to include his research in the Appendix, which contains descriptions of extended sacred works by contemporary African American composers. The Selected Bibliography is intended to recommend additional resources that will provide assistance in planning music for worship.

In the Appendix of Resources, I have included the titles of arrangements compiled in *WOW Gospel Songbook Collection,* an annual publication by various gospel artists from 1998 through 2003. I encourage you to peruse the lists as you plan and select music for your worship services and choirs. Again, "N" Time Music in Charlotte, NC is an excellent source of all of these and many more gospel music compositions.

I am also indebted to my friend and colleague Paul Hamill, Editor of *The Church Music Handbook* published annually by Gemini Press International whose sole selling agent is Theodore Presser Company of King of Prussia, PA. I was introduced to Paul's indispensable and comprehensive Handbook as Minister of Music/Church Organist of the Hartford Memorial Baptist Church in Detroit, MI from 1983-1996. It became my annual guide for planning and selecting music for worship. *The Church*

*Music Handbook* is one the finest and most current resources for planning music and worship in the Christian church to be found anywhere. I am most appreciative for his kindness to share copies from the 1999-2000 Handbook through the current 2002-2003 Handbook with me in preparation for this work which I have incorporated from time to time. It offers suggestions for hymns, anthems, and organ compositions appropriate for each Sunday from September of the current year to August of the following year. The selections, based on the Revised Common, Episcopal, Lutheran, and Roman lectionaries, can also act as a nucleus for finding other hymns and compositions that are suitable and readily available in individual church situations. I highly recommend this annual resource for pastors, worship leaders, and musicians. The current copy of *The Church Music Handbook* can be obtained by writing: Theodore Presser Co., 588 North Gulph Road, King of Prussia, PA 19406, or by calling (610) 525-3636 or FAX; (610) 527-7841. The email address is geminipress@taconic.net.

In his classic book, *Church Music and Theology*, Eric Routley said, "When the minister and musician refuse to communicate with one another...at worst it will be, as it often in practice is, a wicked waste of an opportunity for glorifying God through fruitful partnership." It is my sincere hope and prayer that *Waiting to Go!* will provide an ongoing opportunity for dialogue and communication between the minister and the musician. This "fruitful partnership," so desperately needed, will provide a wonderful catalyst by which the pulpit and the choir loft can more effectively lead the People of God in worship. This kind of planning and collaboration will certainly elevate and enhance music and worship in the African American church to new and ultimate dimensions that please and honor God!

—James Abbington

# Trinity Sunday

**Year A:** Genesis 1: 1-2: 4a/ Psalm 8/ 2 Corinthians 13: 11-13/ Matthew 28: 16-20

**Year B:** Isaiah 6: 1-8/ Psalm 29/ Romans 8: 12-17/ John 3: 1-17

**Year C:** Proverbs 8: 1-4, 22-31/ Psalm 8/ Romans 5: 1-5/ John 16: 12-15

**Appropriate Banner and Altar Colors:** White or Gold

## FOCUS

God has done it again! A new creation has been formed. The Holy Fire of God's Spirit has touched the exhausted, timid and scared folks who were hiding out in the Upper Room. Their waiting and praying together has brought them a cord of unity that they take into the streets. Those who have been filled to overflowing are now prepared to go and tell the Jesus story in the languages of the entire known world. With the coming of The Holy Spirit God has transformed the world again. The redemptive work of Jesus is now sealed in the very beings of these who will testify, convince and win converts to The Way. Holy, Holy, Holy, the Lord God Almighty reigns, world without end. With empowered spirits, embolden tongues and enthusiasm the Church of God is on the go!

### CALL TO WORSHIP

**Leader:** We've a story to tell to the nations.

**People:** We have come to give glory to the Trinity.

**Leader:** We've a story to share with the world.

**People:** Our God reigns!

**Leader:** We've a message of transformation.

**People:** The Creator, Redeemer and Power has our reverence and our worship.

We gather to offer humble praise. Amen.

### ALTAR FOCUS

The Altar can reflect the many creative ways that God has sustained and maintained our world. The Cross of Christ should play a dramatic role in today's visual story, as well as a dove to signify the presence of The Holy Spirit. This is a day that baptisms can work well as the full Trinity appeared at the occasion of John's baptism of Jesus. The emphasis is on the Three-in-one God. This is the mystery of our faith.

# Musical Suggestions for Trinity Sunday

## Hymns for the Day

| Title | AAHH | AME | AMEZ | LEVS | LMGM | NNBH | TFBF | YL | HG |
|---|---|---|---|---|---|---|---|---|---|
| Come, Thou (Now) Almighty King | 327 | 7 | 2 | • | 76 | 38 | • | 16 | • |
| God the Father, Son and Spirit | • | • | • | • | 77 | • | • | • | • |
| Holy God, We Praise Thy Name | • | • | • | • | 193 | 13 | • | • | • |
| Holy, Holy, Holy! Lord God Almighty | 329 | 25 | 1 | • | 78 | 1 | • | 11 | • |
| Let Your Spirit Teach Me, Lord | • | • | • | • | • | • | • | • | 13 |
| O God, Almighty Father | • | • | • | • | 79 | • | • | • | • |
| Praise God, from Whom All Blessings (Bourgeois) | 651 | • | 15 | • | • | • | • | 58 | • |
| Tell It! Tell It Out with Gladness | • | • | • | • | • | • | • | • | 92 |

| Gospel Selections | AAHH | AME | AMEZ | LEVS | LMGM | NNBH | TFBF | YL | HG |
|---|---|---|---|---|---|---|---|---|---|
| Father, I Adore You | 330 | • | • | • | • | • | • | 26 | • |
| Holy, Holy | 328 | • | • | • | • | • | 289 | 186 | • |
| Praise God, from Whom All Blessings (Hatton) | 650 | • | • | 56 | 306 | 559 | 276 | 52 | • |

## Anthems

Psalm 150  *Nathan Carter* (GIA)

**The Church's One Foundation**
   *arr. Roger Holland, II* (GIA)

**O Trinity, O Trinity**  *David Hurd* (GIA)

**Hymn to the Trinity**  *Peter I. Tchaikovsky*

## Organ Music

Prelude on NICAEA  *David Cherwien*

All Glory Be to God of High  *Johann S. Bach*

All Glory Be to God on High  *Johann Pachelbel*

Postlude on OLD HUNDREDTH  *Fred Bock*

# Second Sunday after Pentecost
## May 29–June 4

**Year A:** Genesis 6: 9-22; 7: 24; 8: 14-19/ Psalm 46/ Romans 1: 16-17; 3: 22b-31/ Matthew 7: 21-29
**Year B:** 1 Samuel 3: 1-20/ Psalm 139: 1-6, 13-18/ 2 Corinthians 4: 5-12/ Mark 2: 23-3: 6
**Year C:** 1 Kings 18: 20-39/ Psalm 96/ Galatians 1: 1-12/ Luke 7: 1-10
**Appropriate Banner and Altar Colors:** Green

## Focus

Every scripture cries out, "To whom do I pledge my allegiance?" The life of a child, Samuel, born of the first woman with a recorded prayer in God's Word, is called to lead the people back to God. Hannah's petition comes after years of barrenness and harassment by another sister. Prayer not only changed her life, but brought into the world the first priest-prophet to be used by God. Hope is the metaphor of this day. For we, the Church, always find ourselves saying one thing and living another! Yet, because of the hope that we have confessed in Jesus the Holy Spirit intervenes and we are saved from the folly of our ways. We are invited by God to come boldly before the Throne of Grace where we are promised grace to help us in our times of need. Before we go, make sure we are prayer prepared. For our hope is built on nothing less, than the saving blood of Christ and his righteousness.

## The Call to Confession

**Leader:** Disorder, disharmony and disunity mar both our world and our lives. It is the will of God that we live lives of peace in unity with all. This is our time of confession that the sin in our lives may be forgiven.

## Confession

Gracious and loving God, we approach your Throne with confession. We have sinned. There is no good in us. We want to be cleansed by the blood of Jesus. We long to be filled with your keeping power. Forgive us. Wash us. Empower us. Use us to spread the news of your amazing grace we pray in the Name of Matchless Love.

## Altar Focus

The Altar focus can use the natural elements that sprout and bud, along with photos of young children leading adults in significant events throughout the life of your congregation. Childrens' Day is often celebrated in congregations during this time of year. Graduates and promotions are honored.

## MUSICAL SUGGESTIONS FOR THE SECOND SUNDAY AFTER PENTECOST

### HYMNS FOR THE DAY

| Title | AAHH | AME | AMEZ | LEVS | LMGM | NNBH | TFBF | YL | HG |
|---|---|---|---|---|---|---|---|---|---|
| Blest Be the Tie that Binds | 341 | 522 | 493 | · | · | 298 | · | 34 | · |
| Come, Ye Disconsolate | 421 | 227 | 447 | 147 | 255 | 264 | 186 | 287 | · |
| Great Is Thy Faithfulness | 158 | 84 | 80 | 189 | 242 | 45 | 283 | 122 | · |
| Hold to God's Unchanging Hand | 404 | 513 | · | · | 78 | 51 | 231 | 406 | · |
| I Will Trust in the Lord | 391 | · | 75 | 193 | 232 | 285 | 256 | 333 | · |
| O Master, Let Me Walk with Thee | · | 299 | 678 | · | · | 445 | · | · | · |
| O Thou, in Whose Presence | · | 83 | 454 | · | · | · | · | · | · |
| The Solid Rock | 385 | | | | | 274 | · | 103 | · |

| Spirituals | AAHH | AME | AMEZ | LEVS | LMGM | NNBH | TFBF | YL | HG |
|---|---|---|---|---|---|---|---|---|---|
| I Want Jesus to Walk with Me | 563 | 375 | 514 | 70 | 263 | 500 | 66 | 381 | · |

| Gospel Selections | AAHH | AME | AMEZ | LEVS | LMGM | NNBH | TFBF | YL | HG |
|---|---|---|---|---|---|---|---|---|---|
| I Don't Feel No Ways Tired | 414 | · | · | 199 | 159 | · | · | 364 | · |
| The Storm Is Passing Over | 427 | · | · | · | · | · | · | · | · |
| We've Come This Far by Faith | 412 | · | · | 208 | 225 | 559 | 276 | 52 | · |

### ANTHEMS

Let This Mind Be in You  *Lee Hoiby*  
Lord, Jesus, Think on Me  *John Carter*

King of Glory, King of Peace  *Harold Friedell*  
O Love, How Deep  *Gerald Near, Everett Titcomb,*  
  or *Eric Thiman*

### ORGAN MUSIC

**Invocation**  *George Walker*  
**I Call to Thee, Lord Jesus Christ, BWV 639**  *Johann S. Bach*  
**Melody**  *Samuel Coleridge-Taylor*  
**Prelude on** FOUNDATION  *Paul Hamill*

# THIRD SUNDAY AFTER PENTECOST
## JUNE 5-JUNE 11

**Year A:** Genesis 12: 1-9/ Psalm 33: 1-12/ Romans 4: 13-25/ Matthew 9: 9-13, 18-26
**Year B:** 1 Samuel 8: 4-20/ Psalm 138/ 2 Corinthians 4: 13-5: 1/ Mark 3: 20-35
**Year C:** 1 Kings 17: 8-24/ Psalm 146/ Galatians 1: 11-24/ Luke 7: 11-17
**Appropriate Banner and Altar Colors:** Green

## FOCUS

Oh for thousands of tongues to tell the vast love of God for us! The images of folks with nothing being loved by God; cared for by God's providence; nourished by unexplained blessings and brought into covenant relationship with The Almighty overwhelm us in these passages. God selects two old, barren folks and makes them an outlandish promise of more offspring than grains of sand. God feeds a prophet by providing food for a "heathen" woman and her son so that all three are well fed during a famine. The mercy and tender love of God replenish dried brooks and dried up hopes. This is good news for those going and wondering about provision. This is hope for those with vision and no finance. This is the continuing story of we, who have nothing being called into relationship by the One who owns all! God's faithfulness has no bounds.

## BENEDICTION AND BLESSING

**Leader:** Go into the world as those with a future and a hope.
**People:** We go to tell the wonderful deeds God has done for us.
**Leader:** Go into the world knowing that dried up hopes can be replenished.
**People:** We go with the assurance that even dead dreams are resurrected by God.
**Leader:** Go into the world! The Fount of Every Blessing, The Healer of the Nations and The Sweet, Sweet Spirit enfold us and all that we are called to do.
**People:** We go to be the Church in the world. Hallelujah and Amen!

## ALTAR FOCUS

Celebrate marriages. Celebrate homes. Celebrate politicians. Celebrate God's love for all. In this month of weddings and anniversaries, let the altar reflect a message of family love and family future. Make every Sunday a special, festive occasion to celebrate some group of people in your congregation. Don't forget the single women and the widows and widowers who are often neglected in celebrations. The days are lengthening. Life is inviting us out to enjoy the sun/Son. Just celebrate life!

# MUSICAL SUGGESTIONS FOR THE THIRD SUNDAY AFTER PENTECOST

## HYMNS FOR THE DAY

| Title | AAHH | AME | AMEZ | LEVS | LMGM | NNBH | TFBF | YL | HG |
|---|---|---|---|---|---|---|---|---|---|
| All the Way My Savior Leads Me | 469 | 293 | • | • | • | 236 | 259 | 383 | • |
| Count Your Blessings | 533 | • | 626 | • | • | 325 | 173 | 35 | • |
| Have Faith in God | • | • | • | • | • | 272 | • | • | • |
| I Know Who Holds Tomorrow | 415 | 446 | 48 | • | 187 | 281 | • | 124 | • |
| O For a Thousand Tongues to Sing (AZMON) | 184 | 1 | 21 | • | • | 23 | • | 1 | • |
| O For a Thousand Tongues to Sing (LYNGHAM) | • | 2 | • | • | • | • | • | • | • |
| O For a Thousand Tongues to Sing (RICHMOND) | • | • | 20 | • | • | • | • | • | • |

| Spirituals | AAHH | AME | AMEZ | LEVS | LMGM | NNBH | TFBF | YL | HG |
|---|---|---|---|---|---|---|---|---|---|
| He's Got the Whole World in His Hand | 150 | • | • | 217 | • | • | • | • | • |

| Gospel Selections | AAHH | AME | AMEZ | LEVS | LMGM | NNBH | TFBF | YL | HG |
|---|---|---|---|---|---|---|---|---|---|
| Can't Nobody Do Me Like Jesus | 384 | • | • | • | • | 374 | • | 517 | • |
| God Is So Good | 156 | • | • | 214 | 188 | 395 | 275 | 434 | • |
| God Never Fails | 159 | • | • | • | 224 | 250 | • | 110 | • |
| He Has Done Great Things for Me | 507 | • | • | • | • | • | • | • | • |
| He's Done So Much for Me | 511 | • | • | • | • | • | • | • | • |
| Jesus, You're the Center of My Joy | 491 | • | • | • | • | 530 | • | • | • |

## ANTHEMS

**Great is Thy Faithfulness**   *arr. Nathan Carter* **(GIA)**      **O For a Thousand Tongues to Sing**   *Glenn Burleigh*

**Sing to the Lord**   *Melvin Bryant* **(GIA)**      **Bless the Lord, O My Soul**   *Willis Barnett*

## ORGAN MUSIC

**Rhosymedre**   *Ralph Vaughan Williams*

**Blessed Jesus, at Thy Word**   *J. S. Bach, Marcel Dupre, Flor Peeters*

**Organ Variations on** NETTLETON   *Undine Smith Moore*

**Trumpet Tune in D Major**   *David N. Johnson*

# FOURTH SUNDAY AFTER PENTECOST
## JUNE 12-JUNE 18

**Year A:** Genesis 18: 1-15, 21: 1-7/ Psalm 116: 1-2, 12-19/ Romans 5: 1-8/ Matthew 9: 35-10:8-23
**Year B:** 1 Samuel 15: 34—16: 13/ Psalm 20/ 2 Corinthians 5: 6-17/ Mark 4: 26-34
**Year C:** 1 Kings 21:1-21a/ Psalm 5:1-8/ Galatians 2:15-21/ Luke 7:36-8:3
**Appropriate Banner and Altar Colors:** Green

## FOCUS

God always gets the last laugh! In the Hebrew Scripture, Sarai laughs, but God performs. David is not invited to the house as all his tall and macho brothers are paraded before Samuel the prophet. But, they all have to back up as the horn of oil only pours on David's head, announcing God's choice of the little one as king. Ahab and Jezebel steal from Naboth but the last laugh is on them! In the New Testament, those who need compassion, mercy and help are to be noticed by Jesus. He tells those who want power and position to return to their own as servants! In God's upside down world, where the Emancipation was "hidden" from Southwestern slaves until a year later, God is yet laughing! Today, we celebrate Juneteenth.

## CALL TO WORSHIP

**Leader:** Come, let us lift our voices in praise.

**People:** We come with words caught in our throats.

We have come through a difficult week.

**Leader:** Come, let us join the angels in giving God glory.

**People:** Tears and sadness have made themselves at home in us.

We are weary in trying to do well.

**Leader:** You have come to the right place. For the laughing God is here.

God delights in turning tears into laughter and weariness into joy.

**People:** We long to experience the laughter of God. We will offer the sacrifice of praise and worship.

## ALTAR FOCUS

Pictures of our historical past take center stage. Find pictures that depict the royalty of Africa and those who built the pryamids. Use journal entries that salute our freedom from the fields of cotton and tobacco. Use old letters, old flags and old items of clothing to show the self-definition of a people celebrating slavery's painful past in this nation.

# MUSICAL SUGGESTIONS FOR THE FOURTH SUNDAY AFTER PENTECOST

## HYMNS FOR THE DAY

| Title | AAHH | AME | AMEZ | LEVS | LMGM | NNBH | TFBF | YL | HG |
|---|---|---|---|---|---|---|---|---|---|
| Christ Is Made the Sure Foundation | · | 518 | · | · | · | · | · | · | · |
| Come, Ye Thankful People, Come | 194 | 574 | 243 | · | 205 | 327 | · | · | · |
| Hail to the Lord's Annointed (ELLACOMBE) | · | 107 | 109 | · | · | 272 | · | · | · |
| Hail to the Lord's Annointed (SHEFFIELD) | 187 | · | · | · | · | 272 | · | · | · |
| Hail to the Lord's Annointed (WESTWOOD) | 187 | · | 110 | · | · | · | · | · | · |
| How Great Thou Art | 148 | 68 | 47 | 60 | 181 | 43 | · | 39 | · |
| O Christ, Unsheathe Your Sword | · | · | · | · | · | · | · | · | 94 |

| Spirituals | AAHH | AME | AMEZ | LEVS | LMGM | NNBH | TFBF | YL | HG |
|---|---|---|---|---|---|---|---|---|---|
| Be Still, God Will Fight Your Battles | 133 | · | · | · | · | · | · | · | · |
| God Is a Wonder to My Soul | 132 | · | · | · | · | · | · | · | · |
| I Know the Lord Laid His Hands on Me | 360 | 352 | 52 | 131 | 243· | · | · | · | · |

| Gospel Selections | AAHH | AME | AMEZ | LEVS | LMGM | NNBH | TFBF | YL | HG |
|---|---|---|---|---|---|---|---|---|---|
| All My Help Comes from the Lord | 370 | · | · | · | · | · | · | · | · |
| God Is | 134 | · | · | · | · | · | · | · | · |
| I'll Tell It Wherever I Go | 514 | · | · | · | · | · | · | · | · |
| To God Be the Glory (My Tribute) | 111 | · | · | · | · | · | 272 | 18 | · |
| We Bring the Sacrifice of Praise | 529 | · | · | · | · | · | · | · | · |

## ANTHEMS

**God Be in My Head**  *John Rutter*

**Lead Me, Lord**  *Samuel S. Wesley*

**Amazing Grace**  *arr. Evelyn Simpson-Curenton* **(GIA)**

**A Psalm of Assurance**  *Eugene Butler*

## ORGAN MUSIC

**Amazing Grace! How Sweet the Sound**  *George Shearing*

**Chorale Prelude on** HANOVER  *C. Hubert H. Parry*

**Prelude on** AURELIA  *Joyce Jones, or David Cherwien*

# FIFTH SUNDAY AFTER PENTECOST
## JUNE 19-JUNE 25

**Year A:** Genesis 21: 8-21/ Psalm 86: 1-10, 16-17/ Romans 6: 1b-11/ Matthew 10: 24-39

**Year B:** 1 Samuel 17: (1a, 4-11, 19-23), 32-49/ Psalm 9: 9-20/ 2 Corinthians 6: 1-13/ Mark 4: 4: 35-41

**Year C:** 1 Kings 19: 1-15a/ Psalms 42 and 43/ Galatians 3: 23-29/ Luke 8: 26-39

**Appropriate Altar and Banner Colors:** Green

## FOCUS

Promises! Promises! Promises! The Church goes on the promises that will not fail! There are over 4,200 promises in God's Word. Each of them applies to our lives as people of God. Haggar, a foreigner to God's promise is given a promise equal to that of Abraham! She was enslaved. She suffered at the hand of the dominant culture. She was bred like a brood mare. And, God was there all the time. Because of her faithfulness to her roles and her obedience of submission, she was given a great promise. This helps to explain the unrest in Israel today. God's promises are true and unfailing.

In the New Testament a street woman anoints Jesus. The male host and the male disciples are outraged. But, Jesus blesses this bold woman and declares that the Gospel cannot be preached without her story! We who have been forgiven for our multiple sins know her story! For in the realm of God, it's not about what you own, possess or have earned, it's about being adopted into the royal family by the redeeming blood of Jesus. These stories help us to more clearly see that our God has no respect of gender or race. God is simply a promise keeper!

## CALL TO WORSHIP

**Leader:** People of words come in silence before God.

**People:** We come to offer our adoration and praise.

**Leader:** People of deeds come prostrate yourselves before our God.

**People:** May our lives be acceptable sacrifices of worship.

**Leader:** People of song come with glad thanksgiving upon your lips

**People:** We lift our voices in full agreement that God is worthy to be praised.

## ALTAR FOCUS

Prayer is so much more than mere words can ever express. Let your altar speak to the theme of prayer. This is a good Sunday to show the differing forms of uplifted hands, people lying prostate in prayer, people before the Wailing Walls, even tears as an act of prayer. Burning candles are symbols of our petitions going up before the throne. Let us assist our people with praying with words, only when necessary! Haggar's sitting and crying was a form of petition. The woman kneeling and pouring oil was a prayer of intercession. Do the folks in the pews really comprehend the power inherent in our invitation to come boldly before God's Throne?

## MUSICAL SUGGESTIONS FOR THE FIFTH SUNDAY AFTER PENTECOST

### HYMNS FOR THE DAY

| Title | AAHH | AME | AMEZ | LEVS | LMGM | NNBH | TFBF | YL | HG |
|---|---|---|---|---|---|---|---|---|---|
| All the Way My Savior Leads Me | 469 | 293 | • | • | • | 236 | 259 | 383 | • |
| He Brought Me Out | 509 | • | • | • | • | 49 | • | 432 | • |
| Never Alone | 310 | 441 | • | • | • | 260 | • | 167 | • |
| Showers of Blessings | 571 | • | • | • | • | 350 | • | • | • |
| Standing on the Promises | 373 | 424 | 260 | • | • | 257 | • | 105 | • |
| 'Tis So Sweet to Trust in Jesus | 368 | 440 | 508 | 108 | 236 | 292 | • | 102 | • |

| Spirituals | AAHH | AME | AMEZ | LEVS | LMGM | NNBH | TFBF | YL | HG |
|---|---|---|---|---|---|---|---|---|---|
| Ain't-a That Good News | 592 | • | • | 180 | • | • | • | 171 | • |
| I Will Trust in the Lord | 391 | • | 75 | 193 | 232 | 285 | 256 | 333 | • |
| Plenty Good Room | 352 | • | • | • | 318 | • | • | • | • |

| Gospel Selections | AAHH | AME | AMEZ | LEVS | LMGM | NNBH | TFBF | YL | HG |
|---|---|---|---|---|---|---|---|---|---|
| God Has Smiled on Me | 152 | • | • | 52 | 185 | • | 190 | • | • |
| God Is | 134 | • | • | • | • | • | • | • | • |
| Oh, to Be Kept by Jesus | 423 | • | • | • | • | 212 | • | • | • |
| Walking Up the King's Highway | 402 | • | • | • | • | • | • | • | • |

### ANTHEMS

A Stronghold in Times of Distress, Op. 66   *Joseph W. Jenkins*

Amazing Grace   *arr. Wendell P. Whalum*

My Soul Thirsts for God   *Eugene Butler*

As the Hart Longs   *Felix Mendelssohn*

### ORGAN MUSIC

Amazing Grace   *Jean Langlais,* **or** *Alec Wyton*

Three Pieces for Organ   *Mark Fax*

    I. Freely, hauntingly

    II. Allegretto

    III. Toccata

Allegro maestoso e vivace (from Sonata No. 2)   *Felix Mendelssohn*

# SIXTH SUNDAY AFTER PENTECOST
## JUNE 26-JULY 2

**Year A:** Genesis 22: 1-14/ Psalm 13/ Romans 6: 12-23/ Matthew 10: 40-42

**Year B:** 2 Samuel: 1:1, 17-27/ Psalm 130/ 2 Corinthians 8: 7-15/ Mark 5: 21-43

**Year C:** 2 Kings 2: 1-2, 6-14/ Psalm 77: 1-2, 11-20/ Galatians 5: 1, 13-25/ Luke 9: 51-62

**Appropriate Altar and Banner Colors:** Green

## FOCUS

In most of our congregations, the first Sunday means the celebration of Communion. The Lord's Supper is one where God prepared the Table, invited us to the Table and then gave us the Bread and the Wine to eat from the Table. For all the hungry and the thirsty in the world this food and drink yet suffices for our satisfaction, our strength and our reminder of God's gracious hospitality. As Abraham goes to make a human sacrifice of his son, Issac, he finds that God has provided another meal. The Holy Spirit prompts us to share with one another, it is a sign of our kinship, our family ties and our communion with each other, whether at God's Table or as we gather in all the places where we eat, break bread and remember the One who provides. Giving is the character of God and becomes ours as we grow in Christ. Jesus, the Master Giver, provides new life to Jairus' twelve-year old daughter and makes a wounded woman whole after a twelve-year sickness. Both young and old alike can rejoice because of the generosity of our God.

## CALL TO WORSHIP:

**Leader:** Blessed is the name of our God, Sovereign of The Universe.

**People:** Our God is good and full of benefits.

**Leader:** The Lord nourishes the world, giving food and drink to all.

**People:** The bountiful supply of God's earth is everlasting.

**Leader:** For God's name sake, the people have always been well fed.

**People:** In the Creation, God managed to provide continuing harvests of food.

We join to give praise to The One who sets the Table and invites us to come and dine.

## ALTAR FOCUS

The Communion altar needs a focus of summer fruits, breads and grapes that may come from member's gardens and be used for a repast after worship. Grape vines, wheat stalks and fresh flowers help to create a living altar as they surround the Lord's Supper. This does not have to detract from the solemn tone of this occasion, but does offer additional evidence of God's bounty.

# Musical Suggestions for The Sixth Sunday after Pentecost

## Hymns for the Day

| Title | AAHH | AME | AMEZ | LEVS | LMGM | NNBH | TFBF | YL | HG |
|---|---|---|---|---|---|---|---|---|---|
| As He Gathered at His Table | • | • | • | • | • | • | • | • | 120 |
| As We Gather at Your Table | • | • | • | • | • | • | • | • | 30 |
| At That First Eucharist | • | • | • | • | 134 | • | • | • | • |
| Gift of Finest Wheat | • | • | • | • | 136 | • | • | • | • |
| I Am the Bread of Life | • | • | • | • | 133 | • | • | • | • |
| I Received the Living God | • | | | | 137 | • | • | • | • |

| Spirituals | AAHH | AME | AMEZ | LEVS | LMGM | NNBH | TFBF | YL | HG |
|---|---|---|---|---|---|---|---|---|---|
| I Know It Was the Blood | 267 | • | • | • | • | • | 75 | 253 | • |
| Let Us Break Bread Together | 686 | 530 | 338 | • | 135 | 358 | 123 | 30 | • |
| Were You There? | 254 | 136 | 156 | 37 | 43 | 109 | 81 | 260 | • |

| Gospel Selections | AAHH | AME | AMEZ | LEVS | LMGM | NNBH | TFBF | YL | HG |
|---|---|---|---|---|---|---|---|---|---|
| A Communion Hymn | 682 | • | • | • | • | • | • | • | • |
| Even Me | • | • | 463 | 167 | 138 | 536 | 120 | 416 | • |
| Koinonia | 579 | • | • | • | • | • | • | • | • |
| Lord, I Have Seen Thy Salvation | 679 | • | • | 153 | • | • | • | • | • |
| Taste and See | 680 | • | • | 154 | 129 | • | 126 | • | • |
| We Remember You | 683 | • | • | • | • | • | • | • | • |

## Anthems

**Bread of the World**   *Stan Pethel,* **or** *Gordon Young*

**The Precious Blood of Jesus Medley**   *arr. Joseph Joubert*

**God So Loved the World**   *John Stainer*

**Greater Love Hath No Man**   *John Ireland*

## Organ Music

**Communion, Op. 58, No. 2**   *Louis Vierne*

**Elevation**   *George Walker*

**May Be duh Las' Time, Ah Don' Know!**   *William F. Smith* (**from** *Songs of Deliverance*)

**Bread of Heaven**   *William B. Cooper*

# SEVENTH SUNDAY AFTER PENTECOST
## JULY 3 -JULY 9

**Year A:** Genesis 24: 34-38, 42-49, 58-67/ Psalm 45: 10-17/ Romans 7: 15-25a/ Matthew 11: 16-19, 25-30
**Year B:** 2 Samuel 5: 1-5, 9-10/ Psalm 48/ 2 Corinthians 12: 2-10/ Mark 6: 1-13
**Year C:** 2 Kings 5: 1-14/ Psalm 30/ Galatians 6: 1-16/ Luke 10:1-11, 16-20
**Appropriate Altar and Banner Colors:** Green

## FOCUS

As we celebrate America's Independence Day, the Holy Spirit reminds us how free we are to go and become servants to the world! Free from the bounds of sin, we are now free to be servants to all who need to hear the word of grace that Jesus commissioned us to deliver. A young slave girl speaks her words of grace to the man who had captured her away from her family and country. She tells him about the man of God in her country and he goes to be instructed, "Go and dip in the Jordan River seven times." He hesitates. Again, he is urged, "Go." Healing comes to him. Then, Jesus commissions seventy to "go" and to not become encumbered by "stuff and things" but to take the word of comfort, deliverance and salvation to the surrounding areas. They go, in his strength, with his power and authority. We are free to do the same. The Holy Spirit has gone before us to make our way plain and even smooth.

## CONFESSION

God, we have fallen away from believing in the power of your Holy Word. We read it. We have rememorized parts of it. We can recite it. But, too often we don't believe it will work on our behalf.

Take us back to the days of our hunger for and belief in your Word. Draw us closer to you as we pray and as we worship. Forgive us our sin. We come in full repentence. For this you desire and this you honor, clean hearts that long to do justice in the world. We pray in the name of Jesus, The Christ, who sent us to go into all the world.

## ALTAR FOCUS

The altar should reflect broken shackles. For the theme of being free to do the ministry before us is rightfully celebrated as opposed to "stars and stripes" that have no place in houses of worship. But, we are all freed from the power and dominion of sin's hold on our lives. Photos of the days of slavery can be used to help our young people "recall" the days of The Ancestors who died so that we live. This is another good occasion to decorate with red, black and green so that the history of Black people is not "stuck" in the cotton and tobacco fields of slavery! We had a world, a culture and God before our enslavers came to Africa! Make this a teachable time for every student.

## MUSICAL SUGGESTIONS FOR THE SEVENTH SUNDAY AFTER PENTECOST

### HYMNS FOR THE DAY

| Title | AAHH | AME | AMEZ | LEVS | LMGM | NNBH | TFBF | YL | HG |
|---|---|---|---|---|---|---|---|---|---|
| America the Beautiful | 607 | 569 | 545 | • | 321 | 454 | • | 503 | • |
| God Bless Our Native Land | 608 | • | • | • | • | • | • | • | • |
| God of Our Fathers | 609 | 568 | 530 | • | 322 | 459 | • | 499 | • |
| Lift Every Voice and Sing | 540 | • | 653 | 1 | 291 | 457 | 296 | 506 | • |
| O Christ, Who Called the Twelve | • | • | • | • | • | • | • | • | 55 |
| The Star-Spangled Banner | 606 | 570 | • | • | • | 458 | • | 500 | • |

| Spirituals | AAHH | AME | AMEZ | LEVS | LMGM | NNBH | TFBF | YL | HG |
|---|---|---|---|---|---|---|---|---|---|
| Go Down, Moses | 543 | • | 623 | 228 | 292 | 490 | 87 | • | • |
| Oh, Freedom | 545 | • | 621 | 225 | 298 | 486 | 208 | • | • |
| Walk Together, Children | 541 | • | • | • | • | • | • | • | • |

| Gospel Selections | AAHH | AME | AMEZ | LEVS | LMGM | NNBH | TFBF | YL | HG |
|---|---|---|---|---|---|---|---|---|---|
| Go | • | • | • | • | 66 | • | • | • | • |

### ANTHEMS

**For the Beauty of the Earth**   *John Rutter*

**O For a Faith**   *arr. Nathan Carter* (GIA)

**The Heavens Are Telling**   *Franz Jospeh Haydn*

**The Call   Ralph Vaughan** *William/Paul Hamill*

### ORGAN MUSIC

**Prelude on "We Shall Overcome"**   *Adolphus Hailstork*

**Variations on "America"** (1891)   *Charles Ives*

**A Patriotic Suite**   *Charles Callahan*

**Go Down Moses**   *Fela Sowande*

# EIGHTH SUNDAY AFTER PENTECOST
## JULY 10-JULY 16

**Year A:** Genesis 25: 19-34/ Psalm 119: 105-112/ Romans 8: 1-11/ Matthew 13: 1-9, 18-23
**Year B:** 2 Samuel 6: 1-5, 12b-19/ Psalm 24/ Ephesians 1: 3-14/ Mark 6: 14-29
**Year C:** Amos 7: 7-17/ Psalm 82/ Colossians 1: 1-14/ Luke 10: 25-37
**Appropriate Altar and Banner Colors:** Green

## FOCUS

We owe great praise to God who blessed us with all spiritual blessings in Jesus Christ, and giving us the gift of The Holy Spirit to keep us as children beloved by matchless and non-earnable grace! We have been called, chosen and conferred discernment to discover and use our spiritual gifts in the world. And, one of the greatest gifts is the ability to become an intercessor through prayers. Prayers are more than spoken words. Prayers are many times the deeds we offer in the name of Jesus Christ. The Good Samaritan Story is found in these passages. The "wrong person" became an answer to the needs of the injured who was left on the side of the road by both the preacher and the choir member! Prayer prompts us to respond. We are invited by God to this holy relationship of praying. We did not initiate the pathway to The Divine! It was God who came seeking us, lost in our sin, hidden in our fig leaf designed aprons, as an answer to our unspoken petitions of "Lord, have mercy on us, sinners." David dances as a prayer of thanks. Colossians commands that we become the "go-between" for our communities. Prayer is not an option. It is a privilege to enter God's Throne room knowing that we have been invited for an audience with The One who hears and answers prayers.

## CALL TO WORSHIP

**Leader:** The Spirit of Life in Christ is here to minister.
**People:** Like a strong wind blowing we have been summoned.
**Leader:** The way before us has been cleared, we are free to worship God.
**People:** We are important and special to God!
**Leader:** God so loved us until The Only Begotten Son was given.
**People:** He took on our skin, bore our sin and rose to give us new life.
**Leader:** The Living and Breathing God invites us to live abundantly.
**People:** The Holy Spirit is welcome to usher us into praise and worship as we sing and pray.

## ALTAR FOCUS

The altar can depict many different ways of hands being lifted in prayer and used as answers to prayers. Reaching out, touching and giving are all forms of living prayers. Be sure to include pictures of children who give most freely and unashamedly. One huge photo of Praying Hands says millions of words. Also, the photo from the poem *Footprints* provides images of answered prayers. For this poem depicts us being carried by God during those times that we feel most alone!

## MUSICAL SUGGESTIONS FOR THE EIGHTH SUNDAY AFTER PENTECOST

### HYMNS FOR THE DAY

| Title | AAHH | AME | AMEZ | LEVS | LMGM | NNBH | TFBF | YL | HG |
|---|---|---|---|---|---|---|---|---|---|
| A Sower's Seed Fell on a Path | • | • | • | • | • | • | • | • | 145 |
| Just a Little Talk with Jesus | 378 | 351 | • | 83 | 211 | 339 | • | • | • |
| Renew Thy Church, | | | | | | | | | |
|    Her Ministries Restore | 343 | • | • | • | • | • | • | • | • |
| Sweet Hour of Prayer | 442 | 307 | 446 | 178 | 212 | 332 | 242 | 304 | • |
| The Beautiful Garden of Prayer | 425 | 319 | • | • | • | 334 | • | 308 | • |
| Thy Way, O Lord | 444 | • | • | • | • | 200 | • | 323 | • |
| We Sing Your Praise, O Christ | • | • | • | • | • | • | • | • | 93 |
| What a Friend We Have in Jesus (CONVERSE) | 431 | 323 | 282 | 109 | 214 | 61 | • | 342 | • |
| What a Friend We Have in Jesus | • | 325 | • | • | • | • | • | • | • |
| (FRIEND IN JESUS) | | | | | | | | | |

| Spirituals | AAHH | AME | AMEZ | LEVS | LMGM | NNBH | TFBF | YL | HG |
|---|---|---|---|---|---|---|---|---|---|
| Come Here Jesus, If You Please | 439 | • | • | 163 | • | • | • | • | • |
| Every Time I Feel the Spirit | 325 | • | 220 | 114 | 220 | 485 | 241 | 311 | • |
| I Couldn't Hear Nobody Pray | 487 | 314 | • | 171 | • | • | • | • | • |
| King Jesus Is a-Listenin' | 364 | • | • | 84 | • | • | • | • | • |
| Standin' in the Need of Prayer | 441 | • | 416 | 177 | 216 | 496 | 240 | 310 | • |

| Gospel Selections | AAHH | AME | AMEZ | LEVS | LMGM | NNBH | TFBF | YL | HG |
|---|---|---|---|---|---|---|---|---|---|
| A Praying Spirit | 458 | • | • | • | 213 | • | • | 340 | • |
| Somebody Prayed for Me | 505 | • | • | • | • | • | 246 | • | • |
| This Day | 443 | • | • | • | • | • | • | • | • |
| What a Friend We Have in Jesus | 430 | • | • | • | • | • | • | • | • |
| (ANNIE LOWERY) | | | | | | | | | |

## ANTHEMS

**The Lord's Prayer** *Charles Garner* (GIA)

**Our Father** *John W. Work, III*

**Dear Lord and Father of Mankind** *C. Hubert H. Parry*

**Hear Our Prayer (A Sacred Cantata)** *Felix Mendelssohn*

## ORGAN MUSIC

**Invocation** *George Walker*

**Our Father Who in Heaven Art (first movement from Sonata No. 6, Op. 65)** *Felix Mendelssohn*

**Our Father Who in Heaven Art, BWV 636/737** *J. S. Bach*

**Holy God, We Praise Thy Name** *Adrian Mann*

# Ninth Sunday after Pentecost
## July 17–July 23

**Year A:** Genesis 28: 10-19a/ Psalm 139: 1-12, 23-24/ Romans 8: 12-25/ Matthew 13: 24-30, 36-43

**Year B:** 2 Samuel 7: 1-14a/ Psalm 89: 20-37/ Ephesians 2: 11-22/ Mark 6: 30-34, 53-56

**Year C:** Amos 8: 1-12/ Psalm 52/ Colossians 1: 15-28/ Luke 10: 38-42

**Appropriate Altar and Banner Colors:** Green

## FOCUS

The greatest threat to community in our local congregations is poor self-esteem! Poor self-esteem manifests itself in our pulling down of each other, our refusal to work together and our inability to follow leadership. Prayer is both the need and the answer to this awful dilemma that slows and retards the movement of The Holy Spirit among us. The Romans passage implores us to do the necessary intercessory prayer that will release the spiritual gifts that God has assigned to every believer. When we work in our gift areas we are both blessed and blessing. When we work in our gift areas we can affirm, applaud and appreciate the gifts of others knowing that the whole Body is working together to advance God's Realm on earth. As Jesus visits the villages and the towns he sees the brokenness, the unease, the unhealthy conditions of his own people. He is moved with compassion. The Holy Spirit begins to minister healing to all who need it. The same conditions are present wherever we live today. Prayer releases the God ordained powers within each of us to be freed for the good of all. This is certainly a self-esteem booster!

## CALL TO WORSHIP

**Leader:** The Holy Spirit summons the children of God.

**People:** We gather as the joint heirs with Christ.

**Leader:** Joint heirs share in both the sufferings and the glory.

**People:** Most assuredly, we have done the suffering. We yearn for the glory.

**Leader:** Our present sufferings are not worth comparing with the glory that will be revealed in us.

**People:** We don't even know how to pray for the glory.

**Leader:** But, the Holy Spirit intercedes for us, with groans that our mere words cannot express.

**People:** Spirit of The Living God, intercede for us as we worship with grateful hearts.

## ALTAR FOCUS

Doves symbolize the presence of the Holy Spirit. Discover the many ways that doves are revealed in photos of nature. The creation of an assortment of photos with doves both asending and descending can represent the coming from heaven and returning to heaven with the answers to our prayers. Another image is that of people doing different types of ministry as a means of evidencing that God is glorified in all of our gifts put to use. Sweeping is a gift of hospitality. Singing in the choir or leading devotion are gifts of encouraging God's people. Sewing for others is a form of outreach. Picking up pop bottles and liter is appreciation to God for nature as we employ our gifts of service and help. Typing bulletins is the gift of help. As long as we help congregations to see that whatever we render unto God is both a form of prayer and a means of utilizing our gifts is our primary purpose. Every part of The Body must function as we go.

# Musical Suggestions for The Ninth Sunday after Pentecost

## Hymns for the Day

| Title | AAHH | AME | AMEZ | LEVS | LMGM | NNBH | TFBF | YL | HG |
|---|---|---|---|---|---|---|---|---|---|
| Dear Lord and Father of Mankind | • | 344 | 56 | • | • | • | • | • | • |
| Eternal Spirit of the Living Christ | • | • | • | • | • | • | • | • | 23 |
| Here I Am, Lord | 505 | • | • | • | 283 | • | 230 | • | • |
| Holy Spirit | 319 | • | • | • | • | • | • | • | • |
| In Me | 452 | • | • | • | • | • | • | • | • |
| Keep Me, Every Day | 433 | • | • | 173 | 124 | 310 | • | • | • |
| Lord, Teach Us How to Pray | • | • | • | • | • | • | • | • | 22 |
| Spirit of God, Descend Upon My Heart | 312 | 189 | 224 | 119 | 74 | • | • | 187 | • |
| Spirit of the Living God | 320 | • | • | 115 | 126 | 133 | 101 | 197 | • |
| Spirit Song | 321 | • | • | 118 | 271 | • | 105 | • | • |

| Spirituals | AAHH | AME | AMEZ | LEVS | LMGM | NNBH | TFBF | YL | HG |
|---|---|---|---|---|---|---|---|---|---|
| Come By Here, My Lord | 438 | • | • | 162 | 218 | • | 42,43 | • | • |
| Fix Me, Jesus | 436 | • | • | 125 | 314 | • | • | • | • |
| I Couldn't Hear Nobody Pray | 487 | 314 | • | 171 | 210 | • | • | • | • |
| Steal Away to Jesus | 546 | 489 | 611 | 103 | 319 | 505 | 175 | • | • |
| We Are Climbing Jacob's Ladder | • | 363 | 603 | 220 | 54 | 217 | • | 363 | • |

| Gospel Selections | AAHH | AME | AMEZ | LEVS | LMGM | NNBH | TFBF | YL | HG |
|---|---|---|---|---|---|---|---|---|---|
| A Praying Spirit | 458 | • | • | • | • | • | • | 340 | • |
| I Will Do a New Thing | 443 | • | • | • | • | • | • | • | • |
| Touch Me, Lord Jesus | 430 | 334 | • | • | • | 201 | • | • | • |

## Anthems

**Holy Spirit, Truth Divine**  *Ralph Vaughan Williams*

**Holy Spirit, Dove Divine**  *Koepke*

**Out of the Depths**  *Mozart/Lovelace,* or *Roger Sessions*

**Holy Spirit, Lord of Light**  *Henry Kihlken*

## Organ Music

**Prelude on** CWM RHONDDA  *Paul Manz*

**Meditation (from** *Trois Improvisations*)  *Louis Vierne*

**Meditation**  *Gabriel Dupont*

Con moto maestoso (first movement from Sonata No. 3)
  on "Out of the Depths I Cry to Thee" *Felix Mendelssohn*

# TENTH SUNDAY AFTER PENTECOST
## JULY 24-JULY 30

**Year A:** Genesis 29: 15-28/ Psalm 105: 1-11, 45b/ Romans 8: 26-39/ Matthew 13: 31-33, 44-52
**Year B:** 2 Samuel 11: 1-15/ Psalms 14/ Ephesians 3: 14-21/ John 6: 1-21
**Year C:** Hosea 1: 2-10/ Psalm 85/ Colossians 2: 6-19/ Luke 11: 1-13
**Appropriate Altar and Banner Colors:** Green

## FOCUS

You can not imagine the number of women and men in our local congregations who attend week after week with silent screams, ugly wounds and broken spirits. This week the story of Bethsheba is placed before us. Please take the time to do the work required in earnestly researching the scripture. This is not a story of simple adultery. This is a story of a woman raped against her will. This is the story of the spiritual and political leader who used his power to hurt his subjects, both the woman and her husband. This is the Church's story of Bill Clinton and Ms. Monica! And, rape victims and rapists need our prayers. Both need the opportunity to hear truth and to be healed. Then, the lectionary provides us with the pain of spouses who live with the reality of adultery as told by the Hosea story. Yet, this story is larger than a family tale. It is the true story of God's Church, us, who go in search of other lovers and betray our God. This is a story about the pain that we inflict upon God! These stories call us to the prayer of confession and repentance for our sin. Sin blocks us from being effective.

## CALL TO CONFESSION

**Leader:** This is the hospital of the people of God. There is no story that God does not know. There is no pain that God won't hear. There is no sin too bad to confess to The Ancient of Days. This is our time to come clean and allow healing to claim us. Shall we pray?

## UNISON PRAYER

Great Love, who enfolds the world, we approach you with awe and with conflict. For God we have done so much wrong and so much wrong has happened to us that we find it difficult to put into words. We are both the raped and the rapist. We are both the scorned spouse and the spouse who has betrayed our vows. We are both David and Bethsheba, Hosea and Gomer. Our sin is ever before us. And, our pain will not move. Forgive us our sin. Wash us in your healing streams. Receive our wounds and dress them with your love. Use us in your service to allow others to know just how much you care. We ask and receive your forgiveness in the name of he who has already born our sorrow and made provision for our consolation, Jesus the Christ.

## ALTAR FOCUS

The word for today could be commitment. There are wedding rings which symbolize marriage vows as well as our covenant relationship with God. A wedding is a community occasion and it was the first place that Jesus performed a miracle. Love, as expressed by grandparents and grandchildren, exhibited in the Vacation Bible Schools that are occurring across the city and in family style picnic reunions all evidence our continuing commitment to each other as the covenant people of God. We can only remain in covenant relationship through the binding glue to The Holy Spirit who keeps love flowing. The Holy Spirit travels with us all along the journey.

# MUSICAL SUGGESTIONS FOR THE TENTH SUNDAY AFTER PENTECOST

## HYMNS FOR THE DAY

| Title | AAHH | AME | AMEZ | LEVS | LMGM | NNBH | TFBF | YL | HG |
|---|---|---|---|---|---|---|---|---|---|
| A Charge to Keep I Have | 468 | 242 | 439 | • | • | 436 | • | 330 | • |
| He Brought Me Out | 509 | • | • | • | • | 49 | • | 432 | • |
| I Am Thine, O Lord | 387 | 283 | 433 | 129 | • | 202 | • | 380 | • |
| Love Lifted Me | 504 | 461 | 429 | 198 | • | 385 | 188 | 425 | • |
| Nothing Between | 397 | 451 | 635 | 92 | • | 307 | • | 292 | • |
| Precious Lord, Take My Hand | 471 | 393 | 628 | 106 | 162 | • | 193 | 384 | • |
| Savior, Like a Shepherd Lead Us | 424 | 379 | 278 | • | 47 | 54 | 254 | 385 | • |
| Yield Not to Temptation | 429 | 413 | 518 | 170 | 174 | 244 | 195 | 325 | • |

| Spirituals | AAHH | AME | AMEZ | LEVS | LMGM | NNBH | TFBF | YL | HG |
|---|---|---|---|---|---|---|---|---|---|
| Certainly Lord | 678 | • | • | 132 | 121 | • | 113 | • | • |
| Fix Me, Jesus | 436 | • | • | 125 | 314 | • | • | • | • |
| Guide My Feet | 131 | 386 | • | • | • | • | 153 | • | • |
| I Know the Lord's Laid His Hands on Me | 360 | 352 | 52 | 131 | 243 | • | • | • | • |
| I've Been Buked | 386 | • | • | 195 | • | • | • | • | • |
| Lord, I Want to Be a Christian | 463 | 282 | 606 | 138 | 119 | 156 | 234 | 277 | • |

| Gospel Selections | AAHH | AME | AMEZ | LEVS | LMGM | NNBH | TFBF | YL | HG |
|---|---|---|---|---|---|---|---|---|---|
| Order My Steps | 333 | • | • | • | • | 526 | • | • | • |
| The Reason Why We Sing | 496 | • | • | • | • | • | • | • | • |
| There's a Bright Side Somewhere | 411 | • | • | • | • | • | • | • | • |
| Walking Up the King's Highway | 402 | • | • | • | • | • | • | • | • |

## ANTHEMS

My Shepherd Will Supply My Need  *Virgil Thomson*
My Shepherd is the Living God  *Paul Hamill*
For the Fruit of All Creation  *Hal H. Hopson*
Listen to the Lambs  *R. Nathaniel Dett*

## ORGAN MUSIC

I Call to Thee, Lord Jesus Christ  *Helmut Walcha*
Prelude on SLANE  *Healey Willan* or *David Cherwien*
Theme and Variations on ENGELBERG  *Michael Burkhardt*
Variations on "Kum Ba Yah"  *Michael Behenke*

# ELEVENTH SUNDAY AFTER PENTECOST
## JULY 31-AUGUST 6

**Year A:** Genesis 32:22-31/ Psalm 17: 1-7, 15/ Romans 9: 1-5/ Matthew 14: 13-21

**Year B:** 2 Samuel 11: 26—12:13a/ Psalm 51: 1-12/ Ephesians 4: 1-16/ John 6: 24-35

**Year C:** Hosea 11: 1-11/ Psalm 107: 1-9, 43/ Colossians 3: 1-11/ Luke 12: 13-21

**Appropriate Altar and Banner Colors:** Green

## FOCUS

Both Matthew and John have Jesus dealing with the bread that gives life. In Matthew when the Disciples want to send away the crowd, Jesus commands them to feed the hungry. He goes on to collect the lunch of a little boy, gives God thanks for it and feeds over 5,000 men, not counting the women and the children! If we look at our local congregations and find that the women and the children outnumber the men almost four to one, we see the story as a much bigger miracle than ever before! In John, the hungry people return looking for more physical bread and Jesus begins to give them his own affirmation of who he is: "I am The Bread!" Jesus, the Bread of the World came to die in order that we might live eternally. We have access to this Bread, not only through the ritual of Communion, but through our daily devotion, reading God's Word and communing with one another. Pray to become living bread for those you will encounter this week. For the world is yet hungry for The Bread that satisfies more than empty bellies. We can't go without The Bread!

## CALL TO WORSHIP

**Leader:** The Generous God is present to offer new life today.

**People:** We have gathered, both hungry and thirsty.

**Leader:** The Bread of Life is here to feed us.

**People:** We have come to eat until we are satisfied.

**Leader:** The Well of Life is also available.

**People:** We will drink at the Fountain that will never run dry.

**Leader:** There is no charge for the food and the drink.

**People:** As our offering we bring the sacrifice of our praise and worship.

The Table is spread and the feast of The Lord is going on!

## VISUAL ARTS

Every culture has its own way of making bread, the staple of life. There can be a mighty collage of differing types of bread shown. The wheat stalks and grains will make a festive decoration around a bread maker. For we must also show and teach that there is no salvation without the fires of life! Do not forget pita bread, taco shells, cornbread, skillet bread, crackers and johnny cakes. All of these have helped nations and people to survive.

# Musical Suggestions for The Eleventh Sunday after Pentecost

## Hymns for the Day

| Title | AAHH | AME | AMEZ | LEVS | LMGM | NNBH | TFBF | YL | HG |
|-------|------|-----|------|------|------|------|------|-----|-----|
| Blessed Jesus, Living Bread | • | • | • | • | • | • | • | • | 133 |
| Bread of Life | • | • | • | • | • | 359 | • | • | • |
| Break Thou the Bread of Life | 334 | 209 | 348 | 146 | • | 295 | • | 62 | • |
| Fill My Cup, Lord | 447 | • | 340 | • | • | 377 | 124 | 359 | • |
| Gift of Finest Wheat | • | • | • | • | 136 | • | • | • | • |
| They Came, a Milling Crowd | • | • | • | • | • | • | • | • | 146 |

| Spirituals | AAHH | AME | AMEZ | LEVS | LMGM | NNBH | TFBF | YL | HG |
|------------|------|-----|------|------|------|------|------|-----|-----|
| Let Us Break Bread Together | 686 | 530 | 338 | 152 | 135 | 358 | 123 | 30 | • |
| New Born Again | 362 | • | • | • | • | • | • | • | • |

| Gospel Selections | AAHH | AME | AMEZ | LEVS | LMGM | NNBH | TFBF | YL | HG |
|-------------------|------|-----|------|------|------|------|------|-----|-----|
| God Is | 134 | • | • | • | • | • | • | • | • |

## Anthems

Bread of the World   *Stan Pethel*

I Am the Living Bread   *Michael McCabe*

O Taste and See   *Eugene Hancock*

Eucharist of the Soul   *Lena McLin*

## Gospel Selections

Taste and See   *Kenneth Louis* (GIA)

(See Appendix of Resources)

## Organ Music

Deck Thyself, My Soul, with Gladness, BWV 654   *J. S. Bach*

Deck Thyself, My Soul, with Gladness   *Johannes Brahms*

Impromptu, Op. 78, No. 2   *Samuel Coleridge-Taylor*

Bread of Heaven   *William B. Cooper*

# TWELFTH SUNDAY AFTER PENTECOST
## AUGUST 7–AUGUST 13

**Year A:** Genesis 37: 1-4, 12-28/ Psalm 105: 1-6, 16-22, 45b/ Romans 10: 5-15/ Matthew 14: 22-33
**Year B:** 2 Samuel 18: 5-9, 15, 31-33/ Psalm 130/ Ephesians 4: 25—5:2/ John 6: 35, 41-51
**Year C:** Isaiah 1: 1, 10-20/ Psalm 50: 1-8, 22-23/ Hebrews 11: 1-3, 8-16/ Luke 12: 32-40
**Appropriate Altar and Banner Colors:** Green

## FOCUS

The Hebrew Scriptures point us to the many family feuds that continue today. There is Joseph, thrown into a pit due to having too large dreams for his family. And, there is Absalom who tries to take the throne from his father, King David. David has a crying pity party, weeping uncontrollably over a sinful son. The captain of his army has to come and remind David of his role as servant-leader of the people of God, and tell him to get up and wipe his weeping eyes! Peter walks on water, until he looses his focus on Jesus and begins to sink. Intrafamily "stuff" brings about disharmony, disunity and discord. This is a Sunday to teach families different ways to resolve conflict. This is a Sunday to remind the people of God that families are not perfect nor without fault. This is a Sunday to lead families back to God. Psalms 130 prays for us, "Out of the depths I cry to you, O Lord. Let you ears be attentive to my cry for mercy." This is a Sunday to uplift non-violence within families.

## CALL TO WORSHIP

**Leader:** The Mighty God speaks and summons us.
**People:** From the rising of the Sun to the going down of the same,
        God, perfect in every way, shines forth.
**Leader:** Our God wants to speak and will not be silent.
**People:** We gather to be consecrated as people of The Most High.
**Leader:** God has made Covenant with us and is a promise keeper.
**People:** We join the heavens in proclaiming God's worthy righteousness.
        We pause to worship before The Ancient of Days.

## ALTAR FOCUS

This is a day to proclaim that non-violence is God's way. This is a day to teach different methods of resolving conflict. This is a day to show the "real deal" in families, and not just our smiling portraits that we like to present to the world. Today, put boxing gloves, sabers, rifles and guns on the altar! For weapons of violence are in our homes. Let them be carried out before the benediction and replaced with growing plants, fresh flowers and bowls of refreshing waters. The conflict among us must cease!

# MUSICAL SUGGESTIONS FOR THE TWELFTH SUNDAY AFTER PENTECOST

## HYMNS FOR THE DAY

| Title | AAHH | AME | AMEZ | LEVS | LMGM | NNBH | TFBF | YL | HG |
|-------|------|-----|------|------|------|------|------|-----|-----|
| Blest Be the Tie that Binds | 341 | 522 | 493 | · | · | 298 | · | 34 | · |
| Bridegroom and Bride | 518 | · | · | · | · | · | · | · | · |
| God, Whose Purpose Is to Kindle | · | · | · | · | · | · | · | · | 80 |
| Help Us Accept Each Other | · | 558 | · | · | · | · | · | · | · |
| In Christ There Is No East or West (MCKEE) | 399 | 557 | 230 | 62 | 301 | · | 214 | · | · |
| In Christ There Is No East or West | 398 | · | 231 | · | · | 299 | · | · | · |
| Let There Be Peace on Earth (ST. PETER) | 498 | · | 384 | · | 300 | · | · | 505 | · |
| O Perfect Love | 520 | 545 | 532 | · | 154 | 361 | · | 226 | · |
| Renew Thy Church, | 343 | · | · | · | · | · | · | · | · |
| Her Ministries Restore The Family of God | 519 | · | · | · | · | · | · | · | · |

| Spirituals | AAHH | AME | AMEZ | LEVS | LMGM | NNBH | TFBF | YL | HG |
|------------|------|-----|------|------|------|------|------|-----|-----|
| He's Got the Whole World in His Hand | 150 | · | · | 217 | · | · | · | · | · |
| Lord, I Want to Be a Christian | 463 | 282 | 606 | 138 | 119 | 156 | 234 | 277 | · |
| Walk Together, Children | 541 | · | · | · | · | · | · | · | · |
| We Are Climbing Jacob's Ladder | 464 | 363 | 603 | 220 | 54 | 217 | · | 363 | · |

| Gospel Selections | AAHH | AME | AMEZ | LEVS | LMGM | NNBH | TFBF | YL | HG |
|-------------------|------|-----|------|------|------|------|------|-----|-----|
| Koinonia | 579 | · | · | · | · | · | · | · | · |
| Unity | 338 | · | · | · | · | · | · | · | · |
| We Are One | 323 | · | · | · | · | · | · | · | · |

## ANTHEMS

The Church's One Foundation   *arr. Roger Holland, II* (GIA)

Draw Us in the Spirit's Tether   *Harold Friedell*

The Greatest of These   *Gordon Young*

Keep My Commandments   *Lloyd Pfautsch*

## SPIRITUALS

Give Me Your Hand (from *Three Spirituals*)   *arr. Joseph Joubert* (GIA)

We Are Climbing Jacob's Ladder   *arr. Horace C. Boyer* (GIA)

## ORGAN MUSIC

Variations on AZMON   *Michael Helman*

Benedictus   *Alec Rowley* or *Max Reger*

These Are the Holy Ten Commandments, BWV 678/679 (from *Clavierübung-Part III*) *J. S. Bach*

Prelude (from *Suite for Organ*)   *Adolphus Hailstork*

# THIRTEENTH SUNDAY AFTER PENTECOST
## AUGUST 14-AUGUST 20

**Year A:** Genesis 45: 1-15/ Psalm 133/ Romans 11: 1-2a, 29-32/ Matthew 15: 10-28
**Year B:** 1 Kings 2: 10-12, 3: 3-14/ Psalm 111/ Ephesians 5: 15-20/ John 6: 51-58
**Year C:** Isaiah 5: 1-7/ Psalm 80: 1-2, 8-19/ Hebrews 11: 29—12: 2/ Luke 12: 49-56
**Appropriate Banner and Altar Colors:** Green

## FOCUS

Life is not simply a journey, but a marathon where we depend upon others to cross the finish line! Joseph, dumped in a pit, resurfaces to his brothers' dismay. However, it was God who had sent him ahead for the provision of their lives. A Canaanite woman journeys to find Jesus and her search, although a dismay to the disciples, finds grace and deliverance for her ill child. David dies and Solomon succeeds him so that the journey to Jesus might be fulfilled as he declares, "I am the Bread of Life." Isaiah tells of the Grower who comes seeking lush fruit from the garden, only to find that there are useless grapes instead. For our paths must not only include others, but also evidence justice for every little one along the way. Hebrews chapter of the Faithful, details many who made the journey on our behalf. The baton is now in our hands.

## CALL TO WORSHIP

**Leader:** The God of marathon runners is here with Living Water
**People:** The way has not been easy. We are weary from life's demands.
**Leader:** The God of the weary has come to distribute peaceful rest.
**People:** We seek the safe comfort of The Gentle Shepherd.
**Leader:** The Savior of Zion awaits us.
**People:** God, your smile of salvation will refresh our souls.
We offer the sacrifice of our worship this day.

## ALTAR FOCUS

The race is on! But this is not a distance run, it is a marathon where the baton is passed from one runner to another. This is the metaphor for display. The water stations are the Churches. The pit stops provide the comfort that we seek, and there is fresh fruit for restoration. Show photos of the elders of the congregation during their days of activities, making the way plain for us. Show photos of the infants that depend upon us to leave them a legacy of our faith and faithful stewardship.

## Musical Suggestions for The Thirteenth Sunday after Pentecost

### Hymns for the Day

| Title | AAHH | AME | AMEZ | LEVS | LMGM | NNBH | TFBF | YL | HG |
|---|---|---|---|---|---|---|---|---|---|
| Awake, My Soul, Stretch Every Nerve | • | 230 | • | • | • | • | • | • | • |
| Farther Along | 376 | 355 | 522 | 187 | • | 289 | • | • | • |
| God, Whose Purpose Is to Kindle | • | • | • | • | • | • | • | • | 80 |
| Guide Me, O Thou Great Jehovah (CWM RHONDDA) | 138 | 52 | 82 | • | • | • | • | • | • |
| Guide Me, O Thou Great Jehovah (ZION) | • | 53 | 681 | 62 | • | 232 | • | 31 | • |
| He Knows Just How Much You Can Bear | • | • | 76 | • | 254 | 537 | • | 389 | • |
| Life's Railway to Heaven | 472 | 366 | 555 | • | • | 474 | • | 387 | • |
| Lift Every Voice and Sing | 540 | 571 | 653 | 1 | 291 | 457 | 296 | 506 | • |

| Spirituals | AAHH | AME | AMEZ | LEVS | LMGM | NNBH | TFBF | YL | HG |
|---|---|---|---|---|---|---|---|---|---|
| Be Still, God Will Fight Your Battles | 133 | • | • | • | • | • | • | • | • |
| Over My Head | 169 | • | • | • | • | 488 | • | • | • |
| There Is a Balm in Gilead | 524 | 425 | 619 | 203 | 157 | 489 | 185 | 119 | • |

| Gospel Selections | AAHH | AME | AMEZ | LEVS | LMGM | NNBH | TFBF | YL | HG |
|---|---|---|---|---|---|---|---|---|---|
| Don't Be Worried | • | • | • | • | • | • | 212 | • | • |
| Lord, Help Me to Hold Out | 446 | • | • | • | 229 | • | • | • | • |
| Stand Still | • | • | • | • | • | 519 | • | • | • |
| We've Come This Far by Faith | 412 | • | • | 208 | 225 | 529 | 197 | 395 | • |

### Anthems

O For a Faith   *arr. Nathan Carter* (GIA)

Lord Jesus, Think on Me   *Eric Thiman*

It is Well with My Soul   *arr. Nathan Carter* (GIA)

I Will Trust in the Lord   *Undine Smith Moore*

### Gospel Selections

Speak to My Heart   *Eric Brown* (GIA)

(See Appendix of Resources)

### Organ Music

I Call to Thee, Lord Jesus Christ   *J. S. Bach* or *Helmut Walcha*

Ah'm Trubl'd in Mind   *William F. Smith* (from *Songs of Deliverance*)

I Want Jesus to Walk with Me   Richard Billingham (from *Seven Reflections on African American Spirituals*)

Great is Thy Faithfulness   *arr. Dan Miller*

# FOURTEENTH SUNDAY AFTER PENTECOST
## AUGUST 21–AUGUST 27

**Year A:** Exodus 1: 8—2:10/ Psalm 124/ Romans 12: 1-8/ Matthew 16: 13-20
**Year B:** 1 Kings 8: 1, 6, 10-11, 22-30, 41-43/ Psalm 84/ Ephesians 6: 10-20/ John 6: 56-69
**Year C:** Jeremiah 1: 4-10/ Psalm 71: 1-6/ Hebrews 12: 18-29/ Luke 13: 10-17
**Appropriate Banner and Altar Colors:** Green

## FOCUS

"Had it not been for The Lord on our side, we would have been swallowed up!" declares the Psalmist in reflection on this journey to "go"! For many are the travails of the righteous as we travel. All of one generation dies in the wilderness due to unbelief. A new generation crosses The Red Sea in victory to live in houses they did not build and to eat from vineyards they did not plant. David the warrior King dies so that Solomon the wise can construct a Temple for God. And, Jeremiah, a youth is called to carry God's message of salvation and judgment to a hard-hearted people who refuse to hear. We are called to present our bodies as living sacrifices while discovering that the only way to do it is with the covering of the full armor of God which includes the ability to pray. When we pray, God hears. When we pray, we touch The Throne. When we pray, we are connected to all that heaven affords to enable us on the journey.

We have not been swallowed up, because God hears and answers our prayers. Shiprah, Puah, Jocabed, Mariam, an unnamed Egyptian woman, as well as a woman bent with a spirit of affliction for eighteen years of her journey, all testify to the powerful effects of prayer.

## CALL TO WORSHIP

**Leader:** Weary travelers, come and rest awhile.
**People:** The journey is demanding. The roads are unmarked. We have gotten lost.
**Leader:** The God who journeys ahead of us as Pillar of Cloud and Fire yet leads.
**People:** Often we have tried to outdistance the One who guides our way.
**Leader:** We lose sight of God but God never looses sight of us.
**People:** For The Way, The Truth and The Life of The Journey, we pause to givethanks and praise.

## ALTAR FOCUS

Travelers, with luggage, baggage and provisions make up the symbol for this Sunday. Old, worn pieces of luggage from The Goodwill and Salvation Army speaks on the altar about the many travelers over this road. Trains, buses, airplanes, cars, vans and caravans all signal the ways of travel we have used to pass from one station to another on our journey. This is a good time to feature stories about The Great Migration from the south to all points across this nation. The Diaspora is another story that needs to be taught to our young people and rehearsed for our adults. The journey continues.

## MUSICAL SUGGESTIONS FOR THE FOURTEENTH SUNDAY AFTER PENTECOST

Hymns for the Day

| Title | AAHH | AME | AMEZ | LEVS | LMGM | NNBH | TFBF | YL | HG |
|---|---|---|---|---|---|---|---|---|---|
| A Shelter in the Time of Storm | • | • | • | • | 165 | 267 | • | 143 | • |
| Christ Is Made the Sure Foundation | • | 518 | • | • | • | • | • | • | • |
| Come to Me, O Weary Traveler | • | • | • | • | • | • | • | • | 53 |
| In Shady Green Pastures | 136 | 391 | 641 | • | • | 261 | • | 386 | • |
| The Solid Rock | 385 | • | • | • | • | 274 | • | 103 | • |
| 'Tis So Sweet to Trust in Jesus | 368 | 440 | 508 | 108 | • | • | • | 102 | • |

| Spirituals | AAHH | AME | AMEZ | LEVS | LMGM | NNBH | TFBF | YL | HG |
|---|---|---|---|---|---|---|---|---|---|
| Guide My Feet | 131 | 386 | • | • | • | • | 153 | • | • |
| I Will Trust in the Lord | 391 | • | 75 | 193 | 232 | 285 | 256 | 333 | • |
| The Angels Keep a Watchin' | 130 | • | • | • | • | • | • | • | • |

| Gospel Selections | AAHH | AME | AMEZ | LEVS | LMGM | NNBH | TFBF | YL | HG |
|---|---|---|---|---|---|---|---|---|---|
| Be Strong! | • | • | • | • | • | • | • | • | • |
| I Can Do All Things through Christ | 383 | • | • | 186 | 234 | • | • | 458 | • |
| Lead Me, Guide Me | 474 | 378 | • | 194 | 168 | 233 | 70 | • | • |
| We've Come a Long Way, Lord | • | • | • | • | 294 | 394 | 209 | • | • |

## ANTHEMS

Cheer the Weary Traveler  *William H. Smith*

Come, We that Love the Lord  *arr. Wendell P. Whalum*

Abide With Me  *arr. Wendell P. Whalum*

Lord, Make Me an Instrument of Thy Peace  *John Rutter*

## SPIRITUALS

Nobody Knows the Trouble I See *Fernando Allen* (GIA)

## GOSPEL SELECTIONS

Faithful Over a Few Things *Glenn Burleigh*

If It Had Not Been for the Lord on My Side *Margaret Douroux*

Jesus, You Brought Me All the Way *Kenneth Louis* GIA Publications, Inc.

## ORGAN MUSIC

Jesus, Priceless Treasure  *J. S. Bach, Max Reger*, or *Marcel Dupre*

Pastorale  *William B. Cooper* (from the *African-American Organ Music Anthology, Vol. 2*)

I Want Jesus to Walk with Me  *Henry Sexton*

Toccata  *John Weaver*

# FIFTEENTH SUNDAY AFTER PENTECOST
## AUGUST 28–SEPTEMBER 3

**Year A:** Exodus 3: 1-15/ Psalm 105: 1-6, 23-26, 45c/ Romans 12: 9-21/ Matthew 16: 21-28

**Year B:** Song of Solomon 2: 8-13/ Psalm 45: 1 2, 6-9/ James 1: 17-27/ Mark 7: 1-8, 14-15, 21-23

**Year C:** Jeremiah 2: 4-13/ Psalm 81: 1, 10-16/ Hebrews 13: 1-8, 15-16/ Luke 14: 1, 7-14

**Appropriate Banner and Altar Colors:** Green

## FOCUS

The journey requires rules for traveling safely to our common destination. This is not any old haphazard trip that we are on. We are part of a great host who have already arrived at our destination and await our arrival. The same God who invited them on the journey continues to provide our "burning bush" invitations, when our dungeons shook and our chains fell off! We travel in community so we are taught how to treat each other. Hate evil. Love one another. Be constant in prayer. Practice hospitality. Bless those who persecute you. Weep with those who weep. Associate with the lowly. Do not be overcome by evil. Overcome evil with good. Open your homes to strangers, be on the alert for angels. Care for the imprisoned and ill-treated. Honor marriage. Resist the love of money. Be content with what you have. Remember to imitate Jesus Christ who modeled for us the journey. Winter and death is past on this journey. Blossoms appear due to the renewing power of God's Love for us in Jesus Christ. A new life beckons us to journey one. There is no identity crisis on the journey. Every traveler is an imitation of The Christ life!

## CALL TO WORSHIP

**Leader:** Look! Listen! Our lover is here!

**People:** We have yearned to see him coming, leaping over the mountains and the hills.

**Leader:** The Lover of our souls is like a young gazelle, graceful;

**People:** The bridegroom is virile, like a young stag.

**Leader:** Get ready to glimpse his beauty.

**People:** We are ready to hear the sound of his voice.

**Leader:** Look! Listen! Our lover is here!

**People:** Our lover is here to speak to us with tender words.

We gather in the spirit of praise and adoration to worship.

## ALTAR FOCUS

The last lush blooms of summer should be piled upon our altars. The blossoms of new life, bathed in sunshine are the metaphor of The Song of Songs. We are dealing here with the great appeal of love, which ushers in new life. The animal kingdom is evidence of love and community. African gazelles staged in journey formation, lions in a pride or a representation of the animal kingdom can serve to carry the image of traveling together in harmony, peacefully co-existing together for the sake of one another.

# Musical Suggestions for The Fifteenth Sunday after Pentecost

## Hymns for the Day

| Title | AAHH | AME | AMEZ | LEVS | LMGM | NNBH | TFBF | YL | HG |
|---|---|---|---|---|---|---|---|---|---|
| As a Chalice Cast of Gold | • | • | • | • | 165 | • | • | • | 62 |
| Christ, the One Who Tells the Tale | • | • | • | • | • | • | • | • | 24 |
| Eternal Christ, Who, Kneeling | • | • | • | • | • | • | • | • | 104 |
| Here, Master, in this Quiet Place | • | • | • | • | • | • | • | • | 72 |
| How Firm a Foundation | 146 | 433 | 309 | • | 102 | 48 | • | 54 | • |
| The Church's One Foundation | 337 | 519 | 590 | • | • | 297 | • | 88 | • |
| We Gather Together | 342 | 576 | 28 | • | 307 | 326 | • | 8 | • |
| Where Cross the Crowded Ways of Life | • | 561 | 378 | • | • | • | • | • | • |

| Spirituals | AAHH | AME | AMEZ | LEVS | LMGM | NNBH | TFBF | YL | HG |
|---|---|---|---|---|---|---|---|---|---|
| Guide My Feet | 131 | 386 | • | • | • | • | 153 | • | • |

| Gospel Selections | AAHH | AME | AMEZ | LEVS | LMGM | NNBH | TFBF | YL | HG |
|---|---|---|---|---|---|---|---|---|---|
| Koinonia | 579 | • | • | • | • | • | • | • | • |
| Unity | 338 | • | • | • | • | • | • | • | • |

## Anthems

The Church's One Foundation   *arr. Roger Holland, II* (GIA)

Prayer of St. Francis   *Robin Dinda*

Teach Me, O Lord   *John Hilto*n

A Prayer of St. Francis   *Gerald Near*

## Spirituals

Guide My Feet arr. *Avis Graves* (GIA)

My God Is So High *Courtney Carey* (GIA)

## Gospel Selections

Let the Redeemed of the Lord *Glenn Burleigh*

The Good Shepherd *V. Michael McKay*

## Organ Music

Arietta   *Thomas Kerr* (from *African American Organ Music Anthology, Vol. 1*)

Prelude on LOVE UNKNOWN   *Charles Callahan*

Prelude on MORNING HYMN   *Peter Pindar Stearns*

Deo Gracias   *John Dunstable*

# SIXTEENTH SUNDAY AFTER PENTECOST
## SEPTEMBER 4-SEPTEMBER 10

**Year A:** Exodus 12: 1-14/ Psalm 149/ Romans 13: 8-14/ Matthew 18: 15-20

**Year B:** Proverbs 22: 1-2, 8-9, 22-23/ Psalm 125/ James 2: 1-17/ Mark 7: 24-37

**Year C:** Jeremiah 18: 1-11/ Psalm 139: 1-6, 13-18/ Philemon 1-21/ Luke 14: 25-33

**Appropriate Altar and Banner Colors:** Green

## FOCUS

"All who love God, and are in harmony with your neighbor, draw near to this table with pure faith and receive comfort", intones most hymnals as pastors call the congregation to Communion. Every scripture is about right relationship. The Passover Meal was eaten in communities. No stranger, alien or single person was left out of God's instructions for table manners. Proverbs exhorts us to share our bread with the less fortunate so all may eat and be filled. The Potter shapes us to conform to an image of good will and good works in Jeremiah. And, as the call is to live in harmony with our neighbors, we can be assured that God realized that conflict was inevitable in the Church! So, Matthew gives us the three step grievance procedure we are to utilize for resolution and harmony. In Mark the Syrophenician woman comes begging for the bread crumbs from The Master's Table. Jesus enlarges the Banquet Table to include her and her crazy daughter. And, Jesus both shows and warns the Disciples that in order to be a true follower we must all pick up our cross daily, deny ourselves, love others and dedicate ourselves to going to find, fix and feed those without.

## CALL TO CONFESSION

**Leader:** The call to God's Table is only for those who have gone the extra mile for others and mean to keep doing it. Most of us fall short of following Christ in this manner. There is sin within us and among us.

Let's take this time to confess!

## CONFESSION

God, you know all about us and love us still. You discern our thoughts and are aware of our going out, coming in, lying down and getting up. Before we speak, you know our words completely. You have us hemmed in, we cannot escape your watch. Such tenderness is too wonderful for us to comprehend. Where can we go from your Spirit? Where can we flee from your presence? There is no spot that you are not! We praise you for you created us with reverence and wonder. How precious are your thoughts of us, more than the grains of sand. Yet, we have turned away from you and sin lies within us. Search us and know our hearts. Test us and know our anxious thoughts. Cleanse us from the offensive ways and lead us in the way everlasting. We pray in the name of he who is The Way, The Truth and The Light.

## ALTAR FOCUS

The sign of the dove, representing The Holy Spirit often depicts harmony. If this is Communion Sunday, allow the various types of Communion chalices and patens to be the full display. Photos of children playing, people in both smiling and frowning groups speak to the conflict that we seek to avoid!

## Musical Suggestions for The Sixteenth Sunday after Pentecost

### Hymns for the Day

| Title | AAHH | AME | AMEZ | LEVS | LMGM | NNBH | TFBF | YL | HG |
|---|---|---|---|---|---|---|---|---|---|
| Christ Has Promised to Be Present | • | • | • | • | • | • | • | • | 87 |
| For God Risk Everything | • | • | • | • | • | • | • | • | 26 |
| Let Us Talents and Tongues Employ | 681 | 536 | • | • | • | • | 232 | • | • |
| One Bread, One Body | • | • | • | 151 | 139 | • | 122 | • | • |
| Open My Eyes, That I May See | • | • | • | • | • | • | • | 360 | • |
| Spirit Song | 321 | • | • | 118 | 271 | 326 | 105 | • | • |
| Wash, O God, Our Sons and Daughters | 674 | • | • | • | • | • | 112 | • | • |

| Spirituals | AAHH | AME | AMEZ | LEVS | LMGM | NNBH | TFBF | YL | HG |
|---|---|---|---|---|---|---|---|---|---|
| Calvary | 239 | • | • | 32 | 38 | 110 | 85 | • | • |
| Fix Me, Jesus | 436 | • | • | 125 | 314 | • | • | • | • |
| Let Us Break Bread Together | 686 | 530 | 338 | • | 135 | 358 | 123 | 30 | • |

| Gospel Selections | AAHH | AME | AMEZ | LEVS | LMGM | NNBH | TFBF | YL | HG |
|---|---|---|---|---|---|---|---|---|---|
| A Perfect Sacrifice | 229 | • | • | • | • | • | • | • | • |
| O King, O Lord, O Love | 116 | • | • | • | • | • | • | • | • |
| Precious Jesus | 576 | • | • | • | • | • | • | • | • |
| The Blood Will Never Lose Its Power | 256 | 137 | • | • | • | 146 | • | 250 | • |

### Anthems

Bread of the World   *Stan Pethel*

Eucharist of the Soul   *Lena McLin*

The Precious Blood of Jesus Medley   *arr. Joseph Joubert* (GIA)

Agnus Dei (from *Mass for the World Church*)   *arr. John Worst*

### Gospel Selections

Do This in Remembrance of Me   *Glenn Burleigh*

### Organ Music

Communion (*French Masterworks for Organ*)   *Louis Vierne*

Antiphon III ("I am Black but Comely")   *Marcel Dupre*

Let Us Break Bread Together   *David Hurd*

Toccata   *Eugene Gigout*

# SEVENTEENTH SUNDAY AFTER PENTECOST
## SEPTEMBER 11–SEPTEMBER 17

**Year A:** Exodus 14: 19-31/ Psalm 114/ Romans 14: 1-12/ Matthew 18: 21-35
**Year B:** Proverbs 1: 20-33/ Psalm 19/ James 3: 1-12/ Mark 8: 27-38
**Year C:** Jeremiah 4: 11-12, 22-28/ Psalm 14/ 1 Timothy 1: 12-17/ Luke 15: 1-10
**Appropriate Banner and Altar Colors:** Green

## FOCUS

Woman Wisdom runs the streets, the alleys and the by-ways seeking those who are on the go! She wants to teach them, instruct them and counsel them in the ways that lead to a life rich in Godly success. The Church is on the go to The Promised Land. With enemies behind, mountains around and too much water before them, they panicked. Moses wanted to call a prayer meeting! But God said that success was on the other side of The Red Sea. So, with an angel and Pillar of Cloud and Pillar of Fire before them, they stepped lively to the other side. Our petty games of personal power, fame and fortune don't compare to the glory that Wisdom seeks to instill as we honor, trust, obey and follow God's way to go. It is God's Wisdom that sends a shepherd after one lost, dumb sheep, and a woman seeking her lost "engagement" coin. When both are found, the rejoicing is great and it's time for celebration. The lost has been found. Now we can go!

## CALL TO WORSHIP

**Leader:** Fools say in their hearts that there is no God!
**People:** They are corrupt and their deeds are vile.
**Leader:** The Lord is looking to see if there are any who understand and seek God.
**People:** We come to seek God's face and to learn better how to follow God's ways.
**Leader:** Oh, that salvation for God's people would come out of Zion!
**People:** We gather to rejoice and be glad with our worship of praise.

## VISUAL ARTS

An assortment of different type sheep and shepherds can make their way out of your church Vacation Bible School and Christmas closets to show the "lost" one...way off alone. Women received 10 coins as the equivalence to our engagement rings, when the betrothal was announced. This is a teaching tip if the passage from Luke is selected. Photos of children playing "Hide and Seek" will also help carry this metaphor.

## MUSICAL SUGGESTIONS FOR THE SEVENTEENTH SUNDAY AFTER PENTECOST

### HYMNS FOR THE DAY

| Title | AAHH | AME | AMEZ | LEVS | LMGM | NNBH | TFBF | YL | HG |
|---|---|---|---|---|---|---|---|---|---|
| God of Glory, Grace Revealing | • | 66 | • | • | • | • | • | • | • |
| God of Grace and God of Glory | • | 62 | 227 | • | • | • | • | • | • |
| Help Us Forgive, Forgiving Lord | • | • | • | • | • | • | • | • | 17 |
| Let Kings and Prophets Yield Their Name | • | • | • | • | • | • | • | • | 99 |
| Make Our Church One Joyful Choir | • | • | • | • | • | • | • | • | 1 |
| Only Believe | 406 | 454 | • | • | • | 216 | • | 390 | • |

| Spirituals | AAHH | AME | AMEZ | LEVS | LMGM | NNBH | TFBF | YL | HG |
|---|---|---|---|---|---|---|---|---|---|
| Lord, I Want to Be a Christian | • | 282 | 606 | 138 | 119 | 156 | 234 | 277 | • |
| Shine on Me | 527 | • | • | • | • | • | 62 | • | • |

| Gospel Selections | AAHH | AME | AMEZ | LEVS | LMGM | NNBH | TFBF | YL | HG |
|---|---|---|---|---|---|---|---|---|---|
| Give Me a Clean Heart | 461 | • | • | 124 | 279 | 545 | 216 | • | • |
| How Can You Recognize a Child of God? | 266 | • | • | • | • | • | • | • | • |

### ANTHEMS

My Shepherd Will Supply My Need   *Virgil Thomson*

Sing to the Lord   *Melvin Bryant* (GIA)

The King of Love My Shepherd Is   *Harry Rowe Shelley*

Psalm 23   *David Baker*

### GOSPEL SELECTIONS

Follow Me   *Glenn Burleigh*

The Good Shepherd   *V. Michael McKay*

(See Appendix of Resources)

### ORGAN MUSIC

Adagio (from Sonata in E minor)   *Herbert Nanney*

Aria   *Paul Manz*

Arietta   *Samuel Coleridge-Taylor*

Prelude and March in F   *Adolphus Hailstork*

# Eighteenth Sunday after Pentecost
## September 18–September 24

Year A: Exodus 16: 2-15/ Psalm 105: 1-6, 37-45/ Philippians 1: 21-30/ Matthew 20: 1-16

Year B: Proverbs 31: 10-31/ Psalm 1/ James 3: 13—4:3, 7-8a/ Mark 9: 30-37

Year C: Jeremiah 8: 18—9:1/ Psalm 79: 1-9/ 1 Timothy 2: 1-7/ Luke 16: 1-13

**Appropriate Banner and Altar Colors:** Green

## Focus

"What is it?" The children of Israel are on a journey and the food has run out. Imagine, if you can, over two million people of color, hungry, in a desert, without a Popeyes, KFC, Wendy's or McDonalds! It was pure hell for Moses and Aaron trying to deal with empty bellies, crying babies and whining, complaining adults. So, God rains down manna, the bread of angels. Since it was not salty, greasy or fried, with garlics and leek, the people asked, "What is it?" And, discovered it was the amazing grace of God. God's grace blows us away. Look at the Matthew passage of those who got what they had agreed to, but wanted more since others, who worked less received the same pay! "What is it?" A woman of responsibility, graciousness, means and excellent stewardship is worth great value. She's outside of the home, buying, selling and investing. And, it's a female queen who tells this woman's worth to her son. "What is it?" A woman giving a prophetic word in the Hebrew cannon? It yet causes crying, grumbling and complaining in many quarters. However, only God distributes God's grace! It's all good!

## Altar Focus

Statues of working women would sit well around an altar if the passage from Proverbs is used today. Groups of migrant and farm workers will help establish the fact that what we eat at the dinner table is the result of others' hard labor. Photos of mothers reading to, talking to and teaching their sons, affirms and illustrates the ancient Proverbs text.

## MUSICAL SUGGESTIONS FOR THE EIGHTEENTH SUNDAY AFTER PENTECOST

### HYMNS FOR THE DAY

| Title | AAHH | AME | AMEZ | LEVS | LMGM | NNBH | TFBF | YL | HG |
|---|---|---|---|---|---|---|---|---|---|
| Amazing Grace (MARTYRDOM) | • | • | • | • | • | 163 | • | • | • |
| Amazing Grace (MCINTOSH) | 271 | 226 | 501 | 181 | 173 | 161 | • | 80 | • |
| For the Fruits of This Creation | • | • | • | • | • | • | • | • | 156 |
| God of Grace and God of Glory | • | 62 | 227 | • | • | • | • | • | • |
| My Faith Looks Up to Thee | 456 | 415 | 468 | 88 | 221 | 273 | • | 127 | • |
| The Thirsty Cry for Water, Lord | • | • | • | • | • | • | • | • | 157 |

| Spirituals | AAHH | AME | AMEZ | LEVS | LMGM | NNBH | TFBF | YL | HG |
|---|---|---|---|---|---|---|---|---|---|
| He's a Mighty Good Leader | • | • | • | • | 265 | • | • | • | • |
| I Just Come from the Fountain (His Name So Sweet) | • | • | • | 127 | 110 | • | 111 | 365 | • |
| It's Alright | 526 | • | • | • | • | • | • | • | • |

| Gospel Selections | AAHH | AME | AMEZ | LEVS | LMGM | NNBH | TFBF | YL | HG |
|---|---|---|---|---|---|---|---|---|---|
| All My Help Comes from the Lord | 370 | • | • | • | • | • | • | • | • |
| Ask What You Will | • | • | • | • | • | 258 | • | • | • |
| Christ Is All | 363 | • | • | • | • | 532 | • | 225 | • |
| God Never Fails | 159 | • | • | • | 224 | 250 | • | 110 | • |
| He's So Real | 237 | • | • | • | 227 | 381 | • | 489 | • |

### ANTHEMS

Lift Thine Eyes/ He, Watching Over Israel (from *Elijah*)  *Felix Mendelssohn*

Christ Hath a Garden  *Gerald Near*

I Waited for the Lord (from *Hymn of Praise*)  *Felix Mendelssohn*

I Will Lift Up Mine Eyes  *Leo Sowerby*

### SPIRITUALS

Guide My Feet  *arr. Avis Graves* (GIA)          There Is a Balm in Gilead  *arr. William Dawson*

### GOSPEL SELECTIONS

If I Faint Not  *Kevin and Celeste Johnson* (GIA)          I'm Willing, Lord  *Kenneth Louis* (GIA)

(See Appendix of Resources)

### ORGAN MUSIC

Sonata V, Op. 65  *Felix Mendelssohn*          Toccata on "Amazing Grace"  *J. Christopher Pardini* (GIA)

Melody  *Samuel Coleridge-Taylor*          God of Grace and God of Glory  *Paul Manz*

# NINETEENTH SUNDAY AFTER PENTECOST
## SEPTEMBER 25-OCTOBER 1

**Year A:** Exodus 17: 1-7/ Psalm 78: 1-4, 12-16/ Philippians 2: 1-13/ Matthew 21: 23-32
**Year B:** Esther 7: 1-6, 9-10, 9: 20-22/ Psalm 124/ James 5: 13-20/ Mark 9: 38-50
**Year C:** Jeremiah 32: 1-3a, 6-15/ Psalm 91: 1-6, 14-16/ 1 Timothy 6: 6-19/ Luke 16: 19-31
**Appropriate Banner and Altar Colors:** Green

## FOCUS

On this journey we discover a topsy-turvy world! Things don't always end the way we expect. And, often, the people we expect to be winners end up big time losers! God does not play "fair", but is always just. A poor beggar sits in the laps of luxury as Jesus tells the story, while the rich man begs for a drop of water. A woman made to "pass" by her cousin, becomes the Queen. When his life is threatened, she uses her head to save his! She becomes the "mother" of the nation and has a national holiday in her honor today. When we suffer we are told to sing cheerful songs. When we have done sinful deeds we are to tell about them in open. We are to prefer to be broken in this life in order to be whole in the next one. Fair?

We are called to bless those who curse us and become like Jesus who gave up in order to win! One child promises to do right and does nothing. The other child swears to do nothing and completes the task. Is this upside down or what? When life gives these types of "sucker punches" there is nothing left to do but follow directions and pray."For the fervent prayers of those who live right are powerful and effective!"

## VISUAL ARTS

Take a globe and stand it on its head. Let it talk about a world gone mad. Let it speak to our being called to behave differently than the world. Let the upside down globe echo our reality, God's rule and reign call us to live an upside down life as followers of Christ. This is not a Sunday for "happy, smiling" faces. This is a day to shake up the comfortable pews with God's call to make a difference in our world.

# Musical Suggestions for The Nineteenth Sunday after Pentecost

## Hymns for the Day

| Title | AAHH | AME | AMEZ | LEVS | LMGM | NNBH | TFBF | YL | HG |
|---|---|---|---|---|---|---|---|---|---|
| God, Whose Purpose Is to Kindle | • | • | • | • | • | • | • | • | 80 |
| He Leadeth Me | 142 | 395 | 292 | • | • | 235 | 151 | 391 | • |
| He Understands, He'll Say, "Well Done" | 413 | 487 | 557 | • | 144 | 466 | 172 | 120 | • |
| How Clear Is Our Vocation, Lord | 271 | • | • | • | • | • | • | • | • |
| Trust and Obey | 380 | 377 | 443 | • | • | 322 | • | •334 | • |
| We'll Understand It Better By and By | 418 | 394 | 636 | 207 | • | 288 | 206 | 135 | • |
| Where Cross the Crowded Ways of Life | • | 561 | 378 | • | • | • | • | • | • |

| Spirituals | AAHH | AME | AMEZ | LEVS | LMGM | NNBH | TFBF | YL | HG |
|---|---|---|---|---|---|---|---|---|---|
| Come Out the Wilderness | 367 | • | • | • | 258 | • | • | 465 | • |
| I Want Jesus to Walk with Me | 563 | 375 | 514 | 70 | 263 | 500 | 66 | 381 | • |
| Standin' in the Need of Prayer | 441 | • | 416 | 177 | 216 | 496 | 240 | 310 | ' |

| Gospel Selections | AAHH | AME | AMEZ | LEVS | LMGM | NNBH | TFBF | YL | HG |
|---|---|---|---|---|---|---|---|---|---|
| May the Work I've Done Speak for Me | • | • | • | • | • | 543 | • | • | • |

## Anthems

Let This Mind Be in You   *Lee Hoiby* or *Austin Lovelace*

Cantique de Jean Racine   *Gabriel Faure*

Wash Me Thoroughtly   *Samuel Sebastian Wesley*

Psalm 124   *Robert Shaw* and *Alice Parker*

## Gospel Selections

If I Faint Not   *Kevin and Celeste Johnson* (GIA)

It Pays to Serve Jesus   *arr. Nathan Carter* (GIA)

It's My Desire   *Horace Boyer and Freda Pullen* (GIA)

## Organ Music

Choral Prelude on BEACH SPRING   *arr. Bernard W. Sanders*

Elegy   *C. Hubert H. Parry*

Chorale Prelude: "Give Peace, O God"   *Vincent Persichetti*

Chant de Paix   *Jean Langlais*

# TWENTIETH SUNDAY AFTER PENTECOST
## OCTOBER 2-OCTOBER 8

**Year A:** Exodus 20: 1-4, 7-9, 12-20/ Psalm 19/ Philippians 3: 4b-14/ Matthew 21: 33-46
**Year B:** Job 1: 1, 2: 1-10/ Psalm 26/ Hebrews 1: 1-4, 2: 5-12/ Mark 10: 2-16
**Year C:** Lamentations 1: 1-6/ Psalm 137/ 2 Timothy 1: 1-14/ Luke 17: 5-10
**Appropriate Banner and Altar Colors:** Green

## FOCUS

Our God really is an awesome God! And, our God really is a jealous God demanding absolute reign in our lives! The Mosaic Covenant says that God is the Sovereign and Exclusive God to be worshipped. God took a group of people with nothing and established covenant with them. God delivered them from years of bondage and worked miracles that even the movies had to acknowledge in *The Prince of Egypt*! God fed them with angels' food and made water flow out of a rock to satisfy their thirst. Now, for God's name sake, the people will obey or perish. It's just that simple. Lamentations reveals what happens when disobedience continues. Timothy reminds us that we have been called, chosen, saved, filled and strengthened to go and tell this story about our awesome and jealous God! If this is Communion Sunday, I dare you to see who's missing from The Table at your local church. God invited a select people, but the Matthew parable shows who will end up at that eternal Table and they don't quite look as we expect!

## ALTAR FOCUS

Search for a picture of The Lord's Supper that does not look like the stained glass one! Find one with seriously physically-challenged people around it. Have an art student draw one that shows people from the streets, the hip-hoppers, the ladies of the night and the gang-bangers around the Table. For the Table is not ours. It's the exclusive venue of God! There are two metaphors of banquet tables that might be considered. One is a long table with dressed up people holding forks that are too long to turn around and feed themselves. They are beginning to look weak, thin and angry. The other table has a rag-tag group with the same long forks. However, they are laughing, healthy and looking good. They are feeding each other with the long forks. How does these images work for you and those you go to the Table with?

## MUSICAL SUGGESTIONS FOR THE TWENTIETH SUNDAY AFTER PENTECOST

### HYMNS FOR THE DAY

| Title | AAHH | AME | AMEZ | LEVS | LMGM | NNBH | TFBF | YL | HG |
|---|---|---|---|---|---|---|---|---|---|
| God of our Fathers | 609 | 568 | 530 | · | 322 | 459 | · | 499 | · |
| How Great the Wisdom | · | 91 | · | · | · | · | · | · | · |
| How Great Thou Art | 148 | 68 | 47 | 60 | 181 | 43 | · | 39 | · |
| Immortal, Invisible, God Only Wise | · | 71 | 49 | · | · | · | · | · | · |
| Praise to the Lord, the Almighty | 117 | 3 | 23 | · | 196 | 2 | · | · | · |

| Spirituals | AAHH | AME | AMEZ | LEVS | LMGM | NNBH | TFBF | YL | HG |
|---|---|---|---|---|---|---|---|---|---|
| All Hail, King Jesus | 227 | · | · | · | · | 546 | · | · | · |
| Jesus Is a Rock in a Weary Land | 222 | · | · | · | · | · | · | · | · |
| Ride On, King Jesus | 225 | · | · | 97 | · | · | 182 | · | · |

| Gospel Selections | AAHH | AME | AMEZ | LEVS | LMGM | NNBH | TFBF | YL | HG |
|---|---|---|---|---|---|---|---|---|---|
| Awesome God | 126 | · | · | · | · | 44 | · | · | · |
| God Is | 134 | · | · | · | · | · | · | · | · |
| Perfect Praise | 296 | · | · | · | · | · | · | · | · |
| What a Mighty God We Serve | 478 | · | · | · | · | 547 | · | · | · |

### ANTHEMS

The Heavens Are Telling   *Franz Joseph Haydn*, or *Beethoven*

All That Hath Life and Breath Praise ye the Lord   *Rene Clausen*

All Men, All Things (from Hymn of Praise)   *Felix Mendelssohn*

Psalm 150   *Nathan Carter* (GIA)

### ORGAN MUSIC

Psalm XIX   *Benedetto Marcello*

For He is King of Kings (Second Version)   *William F. Smith* (from *Songs of Deliverance*)

Partita on "Praise, My Soul, the King of Heaven"   *Robert A Hobby*

Toccata (from Three Pieces for Organ)   *Mark Fax*

# TWENTY-FIRST SUNDAY AFTER PENTECOST
## OCTOBER 9–OCTOBER 15

**Year A:** Exodus 32: 1-14/ Psalm 106: 1-6, 19-23/ Philippians 4: 1-9/ Matthew 22: 1-14

**Year B:** Job 23: 1-9, 16-17/ Psalm 22: 1-15/ Hebrews 4: 12-16/ Mark 10: 17-31

**Year C:** Jeremiah 29: 1, 4-7/ Psalm 66: 1-12/ 2 Timothy 2: 8-15/ Luke 17: 11-19

**Appropriate Banner and Altar Colors:** Green

## FOCUS

Jesus tells ten lepers, "Go!" What a powerful word this is to despised people who have been confined, restricted and isolated. Jesus dares to allow these who are rendered unclean, to come into his presence, to stop his travels and to interrupt his planned itinerary as they ask for and receive healing. The Bible says that it is their "going" that they are healed. We can't allow this passage to sit quietly. We can't ignore the implications for those who are in need of The Master's attention. We are blessed as we go into all the world! While the Children of Israel are standing still, whining, grumbling and complaining, they tell Aaron to make them a golden calf. God's wrath is unleashed. When we are not on our mission of ministering we get into serious foolishness! God gets so angry until the words, "I'll wipe them out and start all over with you Moses!" should get our full attention! Moses pleads for the foolish waiting people.

Moses had to "remind" God of the covenant promises! Who is interceding today while we are confined to our buildings, our programs, our pet projects, making them our golden calf? It's a serious question.

## CALL TO WORSHIP

**Leader:** Praise the Lord, Saints!

**People:** Praise the Lord!

**Leader:** Give thanks to our God who is good; whose love endures forever.

**People:** We can proclaim the mighty deeds of the Lord for we are blessed.

**Leader:** Blessed are those who constantly do what is right and maintain justice.

**People:** God remembers us and grants us favor.

**Leader:** It is God who comes to our aid and saves us.

**People:** We enjoy the prosperity of God's chosen, we share in the joy of Zion

And we join with the saints of all the ages in giving God glorious praise!

## ALTAR FOCUS

People leaving hospitals with smiling babies, those with crutches and in wheelchairs with loves ones being attentive is only representative of how the ten lepers might have been moving along with haste. A smiling photo of Magic Johnson, might help in telling the story of how he is smiling now after being declared "free" of the HIV/AIDS virus. Lepers were treated in ways similar to how we ignore and disregard those with AIDS. Could this be a teachable moment?

# MUSICAL SUGGESTIONS FOR THE TWENTY-FIRST SUNDAY AFTER PENTECOST

## HYMNS FOR THE DAY

| Title | AAHH | AME | AMEZ | LEVS | LMGM | NNBH | TFBF | YL | HG |
|---|---|---|---|---|---|---|---|---|---|
| Banned and Banished by their Neighbors | • | • | • | • | • | • | • | • | 7 |
| For the Beauty of the Earth | • | 578 | 6 | • | • | 8 | • | • | • |
| Go, My Children, with My Blessing | • | • | • | • | • | • | 161 | • | • |
| Let All the People Praise Thee | • | 58 | • | • | 83 | 11 | • | 14 | • |
| Now Thank We All Our God | • | 573 | 22 | • | 208 | 330 | • | • | • |
| We Come, O Christ, to You | • | • | • | • | • | • | • | • | 6 |

| Spirituals | AAHH | AME | AMEZ | LEVS | LMGM | NNBH | TFBF | YL | HG |
|---|---|---|---|---|---|---|---|---|---|
| Do, Lord, Remember Me | • | • | 516 | 164 | • | 508 | 178 | 73 | • |
| I Couldn't Hear Nobody Pray | 487 | 314 | • | 171 | 210 | • | • | • | • |
| I Want Jesus to Walk with Me | 563 | 375 | 514 | 70 | 263 | 500 | 66 | 381 | • |

| Gospel Selections | AAHH | AME | AMEZ | LEVS | LMGM | NNBH | TFBF | YL | HG |
|---|---|---|---|---|---|---|---|---|---|
| Even Me | 157 | • | 463 | 167 | 138 | 536 | 120 | 416 | • |

## ANTHEMS

Behold Now, Bless the Lord   *David Hurd*

Psalm 66   *Walter Pelz*

A Hymn of Praise to the Creator   *Eric Thiman*

Bless the Lord, O My Soul   *Willis Barnett*

## GOSPEL SELECTIONS

Agnus Dei (Lamb of God) from *Alpha Mass*   *Glenn Burleigh*

Stop By, Lord   *Doris Wesley Bettis* (GIA)

The Potter's House   *V. Michael McKay*

## ORGAN MUSIC

There is a Balm in Gilead   *David Hurd*

The Lord Will Make a Way Somehow   *arr. Henry Sexton*

If Thou But Suffer God to Guide Thee, BWV 642/647   *J. S. Bach*

O Master, Let Me Walk with Thee   *Noel DaCosta (African-American Organ Music Anthology, Vol. 3)*

# TWENTY-SECOND SUNDAY IN PENTECOST
## OCTOBER 16-OCTOBER 22

**Year A:** Exodus 33: 12-23/ Psalm 99/ 1 Thessalonians 1: 1-10/ Matthew 22: 15-22

**Year B:** Job 38: 1-7, 34-41/ Psalm 104: 1-9, 24, 35c/ Hebrews 5: 1-10/ Mark 10: 35-45

**Year C:** Jeremiah 31: 27-34/ Psalm 119: 97-104/ 2 Timothy 3: 14—4:5/ Luke 18:1-8

**Appropriate Banner and Altar Colors:** Green

## FOCUS

"Show me your glory, God," is the request Moses asks of God who has appointed him to go back down the mountain and deal with the covenant-breaking, idol-building, whining group of "children" in the Wilderness of Sin! Moses wants some assurance that God is present and accounted for in every move of the journey. His persistence pays off. Jesus picks this persistent attitude up and tells a story of a woman in Luke who has been named, "The Persistent Woman." This is a woman without the normal and customary safeguards of spouse or sons to intervene on her behalf. She is a woman seemingly without resources. She wants what God wants for all of us, justice. The judge is not concerned, but ignores this woman. He is named and called, "The Unjust Judge." He sounds like an evil man with no intent of changing, being transformed or converted. He goes so far as to brag, "I don't care about God or people"! But, the woman does not back off. She won't relent. She won't quit asking for justice. She is persistent and she sees God's glory! And, Jesus tells the listening crowd that this is to be our benchmark as we go! Were you listening?

## CALL TO WORSHIP

**Leader:** Thanksgivings are due our God.

**People:** We will tell the world what God has done.

**Leader:** Sing joyous songs, let the anthems ring.

**People:** Our hymns of praise will translate God's wonder into music.

**Leader:** Let's honor God with our hallelujahs!

**People:** We seek the glory of God for the sake of our souls.

**Leader:** Be on the alert for God in this worship.

**People:** God's wonders, miracles and deeds demand our praise.

## ALTAR FOCUS

Display the scales of justice as a mere sign of what God sends our way when we are earnest in our prayers. Photos of "determined" men, women and children will help the congregation view The Persistent Woman as she sought, demanded and was granted justice.

# Musical Suggestions for The Twenty-Second Sunday after Pentecost

## Hymns for the Day

| Title | AAHH | AME | AMEZ | LEVS | LMGM | NNBH | TFBF | YL | HG |
|---|---|---|---|---|---|---|---|---|---|
| Crown Him with Many Crowns | 288 | 174 | 199 | · | 68 | · | · | · | · |
| Higher Ground | 419 | 347 | 645 | 165 | · | 222 | · | 354 | · |
| O Jesus, I Have Promised | · | 280 | 472 | · | · | · | · | · | · |
| Pass Me Not, O Gentle Savior | 435 | 272 | 291 | 139 | 179 | 181 | 150 | 276 | · |
| Rock of Ages | 559 | 328 | 170 | · | 51 | 254 | · | 91 | · |
| Thine Is the Glory | · | 157 | 194 | · | · | · | · | · | · |

| Spirituals | AAHH | AME | AMEZ | LEVS | LMGM | NNBH | TFBF | YL | HG |
|---|---|---|---|---|---|---|---|---|---|
| Certainly Lord | 678 | · | · | 132 | 121 | · | 113 | · | · |
| I Shall Not Be Moved | 479 | · | · | · | 276 | · | 147 | 351 | · |
| I Wanna Be Ready | 600 | · | 607 | 7 | · | · | 41 | · | · |
| Remember Me | 434 | · | · | 179 | 209 | · | · | · | · |

| Gospel Selections | AAHH | AME | AMEZ | LEVS | LMGM | NNBH | TFBF | YL | HG |
|---|---|---|---|---|---|---|---|---|---|
| Ask What You Will | · | · | · | · | · | 258 | · | · | · |

## Anthems

The Lord God Reigneth  *Johann Pachelbel*

Old Hundredth Psalm Tune  *Ralph Vaughan Williams*

Praise Ye the Lord  *John Rutter*

God is My Rock  *Allen Pote*

## Spirituals

Nobody Knows the Trouble I See  *arr. Fernando Allen* (GIA)

## Gospel Selections

I Have a God  *V. Michael McKay*

There Is a King on the Throne  (from *Alpha Mass*) *Glenn Burleigh*

You Shall Be Free Indeed  (from *Born to Die*) *Glenn Burleigh*

## Organ Music

OLD HUNDREDTH  *David Cherwein*

OLD HUNDREDTH  *Johann Gottfried Walther*

Prelude on OLD HUNDREDTH  *Fred Bock*

Thou Art the Rock  *Henri Mulet*

# TWENTY-THIRD SUNDAY AFTER PENTECOST
## OCTOBER 23-OCTOBER 29

**Year A:** Deuteronomy 34: 1-12/ Psalm 90: 1-6, 13-17/ 1 Thessalonians 2: 1-8/ Matthew 22: 34-46

**Year B:** Job 42: 1-6, 10-17/ Psalm 34: 1-8, 19-22/ Hebrews 7: 23-28/ Mark 10: 46-52

**Year C:** Joel 2: 23-32/ Psalm 65/ 2 Timothy 4: 6-8, 16-18/ Luke 18: 9-14

**Appropriate Banner and Altar Colors:** Green

## FOCUS

"Let me see!" This is the request of the Blind Man to Jesus. "Let me see!" This is the request of each one of us on the journey. The Blind Man was not physically in a position to look around for himself. The Blind Man had to depend on others to tell him what was happening, and, the Blind Man had common sense to ask for the help that he needed. Bartimaeus is us! He is a person with a need seeking The One who can allow him to the ability to look at things for himself. God used Moses to allow the world to "see" what deliverance looked like. They saw and did not believe. Moses delivers them to The Promised Land, but dies without entering into it himself. Job demanded an audience to "see" God. When God shows up with hard questions, Job finds himself seeing himself in a different light. When we can fully "see" the goodness of God, early rain, plentiful grain, wine and oil, we will give thanks, unlike the blind Pharisee, but with humility, like the tax collector. On the journey, we need the power of The Holy Spirit to help us to see.

## RESPONSIVE READING

(BASED ON PSALM 90 )

**Leader:** God teach us how to live the abundant life!

**People:** We want to know how to live wisely and well.

**Leader:** God, how long do we have to wait in order to see?

**People:** Sovereign, please treat us with grace and dignity we pray.

**Leader:** We pray for the surprise of love and acceptance.

**People:** We would sing, shout, laugh and rejoice all the days of our lives!

**Leader:** We long for the days of acceptance to be as many as our days of rejection!

**People:** We yearn for the ability to see the best side of life.

**Leader:** We'd like to experience what you're best at doing,

**People:** Blessing us, prospering the work of our hands and giving our children long life without drugs, violence and death. Have mercy upon us, O God. And, prosper for us the works of our hands so that our children will make you their God!

## ALTAR FOCUS

This is a Sunday when an assortment of crystal candles can be utilized to symbolize the power of one candle shining against the power of no sight. One photo of a single candle on the overhead will carry the metaphor, "Let me see!"

# MUSICAL SUGGESTIONS FOR THE TWENTY-THIRD SUNDAY AFTER PENTECOST

## HYMNS FOR THE DAY

| Title | AAHH | AME | AMEZ | LEVS | LMGM | NNBH | TFBF | YL | HG |
|---|---|---|---|---|---|---|---|---|---|
| Be Thou My Vision | • | 281 | 461 | • | • | • | • | • | • |
| In Me | 452 | • | • | • | • | • | • | • | • |
| Look and Live | 503 | 215 | • | • | • | • | • | 428 | • |
| O Love That Wilt Not Let Me Go | • | 302 | 279 | • | • | 210 | • | • | • |
| Open My Eyes, That I May See | • | 285 | • | • | • | 218 | 98 | 360 | • |
| Take My Life, and Let It Be | • | 292 | 470 | • | • | 213 | • | 337 | • |
| Thy Way, O Lord | 444 | 311 | • | • | 39 | 200 | • | 323 | • |

| Spirituals | AAHH | AME | AMEZ | LEVS | LMGM | NNBH | TFBF | YL | HG |
|---|---|---|---|---|---|---|---|---|---|
| Hear Me Praying | • | • | • | • | • | 502 | • | • | • |
| I'm Gonna Live So God Can Use Me | • | 358 | • | • | • | • | • | • | • |
| Lord, I Want to Be a Christian | 463 | 282 | 606 | 138 | 119 | 156 | 234 | 277 | • |
| Standin' in the Need of Prayer | 441 | • | 416 | 177 | 216 | 496 | 240 | 310 | • |

| Gospel Selections | AAHH | AME | AMEZ | LEVS | LMGM | NNBH | TFBF | YL | HG |
|---|---|---|---|---|---|---|---|---|---|
| Acceptable to You | 390 | • | • | • | • | • | • | • | • |
| I Love the Lord, He Heard My Cry | 395 | 313 | • | 67 | 238 | • | • | 53 | • |

## ANTHEMS

Lord, Our Dwelling Place   *Eugene Butler*
Thy Word is a Lantern unto My Feet   *Leo Sowerby*
A Canticle of Light   *Richard Purvis*
I Will Lift Up Eyes   *Daniel Moe*

## GOSPEL SELECTIONS

As Far As You Can See   *Fred Nelson, III*
Before I Tell Them   *V. Michael McKay*

## ORGAN MUSIC

Hold Out Your Light!   *William F. Smith (Songs of Deliverance)*
Be Thou My Vision   *arr. Dale Wood*
Be Thou My Vision   *Paul Manz*
Toccatina   *William B. Cooper*

# Twenty-Fourth Sunday after Pentecost
## October 30–November 5

## Reformation Day

The last Sunday in October is Reformation Day. On Reformation Day we recall and remember Martin Luther, who rebelled against the Catholic Church's ability to "charge" for the granting of absolution for sin!

He declared that grace was free! His protests were nailed to doors of churches in his area. This gives us the name Protestants. This is a good Sunday to teach the history of The Ancestors who did the work to provide the place where you worship. Their labors of love and personal sacrifices need be uplifted.

**Year A:** Joshua 3: 7-17/ Psalm 107: 1-7, 33-37/ 1 Thessalonians 2: 9-13/ Matthew 23: 1-12
**Year B:** Ruth 1: 1-18/ Psalm 146/ Hebrews 9: 11-14/ Mark 12: 28-34
**Year C:** Habakkuk 1: 1-4, 2: 1-4/ Psalm 119: 137-144/ 2 Thessalonians 1: 1-4, 11-12/ Luke 19: 1-10
**Appropriate Banner and Altar Colors:** Green

## Focus

Moses dies and Joshua is charged with leading the people forward. A famine in Moab, sends Naomi and Ruth to The City of Bread, seeking bread. Habakkuk, challenges God, in the midst of all the injustice around him with the question, "How long?" All of these characters find themselves as those who live by their faith. Joshua leads the people across the Jordan. Finally, they inherit The Promised Land. It's time for reformation. Ruth, a foreigner, decides to follow her Jewish mother-in-law and covenants to never leave her nor forsake her unto death. It's time for reformation. God tells Habakkuk that affliction is coming, people will be running and he is to write the plain truth for all on the journey to note. It's time for reformation. For reformation means change. Reformation means trans-formation. Reformation means living by faith that The Holy Spirit knows the way to lead, guide and direct us as we move forward, on the journey of go!

## Call to Worship

**Leader:** The fall is fully in season.  The cherry trees and strawberry patches have stopped blooming.
**People:** The last apples have worms and the wheat fields are bare.
**Leader:** The days of harvest are almost over.
**People:** Animals are being herded for the winter's cold.
**Leader:** It seems as if life in nature is dying.
**People:** The media portrays death all around us too.
**Leader:** Why would you come to worship on a day of gloom?
**People:** We come to sing our praise to The God of Life.

We come with grateful hearts to the Encore God. For what we cannot see does not matter. God is not dead! We, like the deer are going to the high places. We are not afraid. We dare to worship, sing and give God our praise.

## Altar Focus

"Don't force me to leave you; don't make me go home. Where you go, I go; and where you live, I'll live. Your people are my people, your God is my God; where you die, I'll die, and that's where I'll be buried, so help me God not even death itself is going to come between us." (Ruth 1:16-17) This is the covenant Ruth made to her mother-in-law who had changed her name to "Bitter." We use this in our wedding ceremonies, which are true signs of our being transformed and changed! How can you depict a solemn promise is the challenge of this week.

## MUSICAL SUGGESTIONS FOR THE TWENTY-FOURTH SUNDAY AFTER PENTECOST

### HYMNS FOR THE DAY

| Title | AAHH | AME | AMEZ | LEVS | LMGM | NNBH | TFBF | YL | HG |
|---|---|---|---|---|---|---|---|---|---|
| A Mighty Fortress Is Our God | 124 | 54 | • | • | • | 37 | 133 | 144 | • |
| How Firm a Foundation | 146 | 433 | 309 | • | 102 | 48 | • | 54 | • |
| Love Divine, All Loves Excelling | 440 | 455 | 274 | • | • | 65 | • | 38 | • |
| O Worship the King | • | 12 | 4 | • | • | 6 | • | 3 | • |
| The Call Is Clear and Simple | • | • | • | • | • | • | • | • | 58 |
| The Church's One Foundation | 337 | 519 | 304 | • | • | 297 | • | • | • |
| The Solid Rock | 385 | • | • | • | • | 274 | • | 103 | • |
| The Virtue of Humility | • | • | • | • | • | • | • | • | 132 |

| Spirituals | AAHH | AME | AMEZ | LEVS | LMGM | NNBH | TFBF | YL | HG |
|---|---|---|---|---|---|---|---|---|---|
| I Know I've Been Changed | • | 357 | • | • | • | • | • | • | • |
| Jesus Is a Rock in a Weary Land | 222 | • | • | • | • | • | • | • | • |
| Old Ship of Zion! | • | • | • | • | • | 534 | • | • | • |
| 'Tis the Ol' Ship of Zion | 349 | • | 612 | • | • | • | 199 | 494 | • |

### ANTHEMS

O How Amiable   *William Mathias*

Psalm 46   *John Ness Beck*

A Mighty Fortress is Our God   *Carl F. Mueller*

Psalm 46 - God is Our Refuge and Strength   *John Weaver*

### SPIRITUALS

Jesus Is a Rock in a Weary Land *arr. Glenn Burleigh*

My Soul's Been Anchored in the Lord *arr. Charles Garner* (GIA)

My Soul's Been Anchored in the Lord *arr. Glenn Jones*

### GOSPEL SELECTIONS

All Hail the Power of Jesus' Name *arr. Sean T. Deveaux*     Credo (I Believe in God) from *Gospel Mass  Robert Ray*

O Worship the King *arr. Wendell Woods* (GIA)

### ORGAN MUSIC

EIN FESTE BERG   *David Cherwein*        EIN FESTE BERG   *Charles Callahan*

EIN FESTE BERG   *Dietrich Buxtehude*      EIN FESTE BERG , BWV 720   *J. S. Bach*

EIN FESTE BERG   *Gerald Near*

# Twenty-Fifth Sunday after Pentecost
## November 1 or First Sunday in November
## All Saints Day

**Year A:** Revelation 7: 9-17/ Psalm 34: 1-10, 22/ 1 John 3: 1-3/ Matthew 5: 1-12
**Year B:** Isaiah 25: 6-9/ Psalm 24/ Revelation 21: 1-6a/ John 11: 32-44
**Year C:** Daniel 7: 1-3, 15-18/ Psalm 149/ Ephesians 1: 11-23/ Luke 6: 20-31
**Appropriate Banner and Altar Colors:** White or Gold

## Focus

"Amen! Blessing and glory and wisdom, thanksgiving and honor and power and might, be to our God forever and ever. Amen!" This is the hymn of the saints who have crossed over into eternity. This is their chorus, along with the the elders, the four living creatures and the multitudes who have come through great tribulation, washed their robes in the blood of the Lamb and worship before God's Throne. This is the vision that John, The Revelator was given while on his journey of go, banished to the Isle of Patmos. What the political powers had meant for evil, God turned it to good for both John and The Church. For now we have a picture of what our loved ones, missing from among us, are awaiting. They don't want to return to this vale of sorrow. We don't cry for them. We cry because we miss their physical tabernacle. But they are with God who has promised to wipe away every tear from their eye for they will never experience death, sorrow or crying nor pain. There, everything is bright and new! Let's wipe our weeping eyes and be steadfast on the journey to join them over there!

## Call to Confession

**Leader:** Too many of us remain in our own personal tombs while Jesus has called us to come forth. The power of death has to give way to the new life in Jesus Christ. For those of us afraid to come forth, let us pray.

## Confession

Light of Life, my comfortable tomb has become alright with me. Like Lazurus, I have heard the call.

But, I have stayed wrapped up in my sin. I have allowed death to reign in me. Free me from my unclean state. Forgive me. Wash me and fill me with The Holy Sprit's power of new life, I pray in the name of The One who turns graveyards into parties, Jesus The Christ.

## Altar Focus

On your altar, set up identical short stubby candles to represent each person who has died in your congregation. The month before, the church clerk should provide a printed page of the list of names recorded in your office of all those who have died during the year, since last November 1. You might want to advertise for the names of loved ones among members, whose funerals were in other places. The idea is to leave no ones loved one off your roll. The candles, in plain holders, should surround the altar candles and the Communion elements. For this is the picture of The Heavenly Banquet where Jesus Christ will feed us all! As the pastor or liturgist calls each name, let the organ peal a note, while the candle for them is lit from the altar candles. If this is done right after the call the worship, the first hymn can be *For All The Saints*. The candles will last throughout the worship experience.

## Musical Suggestions for The Twenty-Fifth Sunday after Pentecost

### Hymns for the Day

| Title | AAHH | AME | AMEZ | LEVS | LMGM | NNBH | TFBF | YL | HG |
|---|---|---|---|---|---|---|---|---|---|
| For All the Saints | 339 | 476 | 578 | • | 105 | 301 | • | • | • |
| Martha, Mary, Waiting, Weeping | • | • | • | • | • | • | • | • | 102 |
| O God, Our Help in Ages Past | 170 | 61 | 81 | • | 230 | 46 | • | 15 | • |
| The Crown | 604 | • | • | • | • | • | • | • | • |
| Wear a Crown | 603 | • | • | • | • | • | • | • | • |
| When the Roll is Called Up Yonder | 191 | 497 | • | • | • | 481 | • | • | • |
| When We All Get to Heaven | 594 | 511 | 560 | 20 | • | 468 | • | 170 | • |

| Spirituals | AAHH | AME | AMEZ | LEVS | LMGM | NNBH | TFBF | YL | HG |
|---|---|---|---|---|---|---|---|---|---|
| I Want to Die Easy | • | 357 | • | • | • | • | • | • | • |
| In Bright Mansions | 222 | • | • | • | • | • | • | • | • |

| Gospel Selections | AAHH | AME | AMEZ | LEVS | LMGM | NNBH | TFBF | YL | HG |
|---|---|---|---|---|---|---|---|---|---|
| We Shall Behold Him | 583 | • | • | • | • | • | • | • | • |
| When the Saints Go Marching In | 595 | • | • | • | • | • | 180 | • | • |

### Anthems

The Souls of the Righteous  *T. Tertius Noble*
For the Feast of All Saints  *Gerald Near*
How Lovely is Thy Dwelling Place  *Johannes Brahms*
Blessed Are They that Dwell in Thy House  *Jean Berger*

### Spirituals

I Want to Die Easy  *arr. Roland M. Carter*
In Bright Mansions  *arr. Roland M. Carter*
Lazarus  *Robert Tanner* (GIA)

### Gospel Selections

Anticipation  *V. Michael McKay*
Don't Cry  *Kirk Franklin/Richard Smallwood*
(See Appendix of Resources)

### Organ Music

Cortege et Litanie  *Marcel Dupre*
Litany for All Saints  *Schubert/arr. Raymond H. Herbek*
Prelude on SINE NOMINE  *Ralph Vaughan Williams*
Jerusalem, My Happy Home  *George Shearing*
Great Day, dud Righteous Marchin'!  *William F. Smith (Songs of Deliverance)*

# Twenty-Sixth Sunday after Pentecost
## November 6 - November 12

**Year A:** Joshua 24: 1-3a, 14-25/ Psalm 78: 1-7/ 1 Thessalonians 4: 13-18/ Matthew 25: 1-13
**Year B:** Ruth 3: 1-5; 4: 13-17/ Psalm 127/ Hebrews 9: 24-28/ Mark 12: 38-44
**Year C:** Haggai 1: 15b—2:9/ Psalm 145: 1-5, 17-21/ 2 Thessalonians 2: 1-5, 13-17/ Luke 20: 27-38
**Appropriate Banner and Altar Colors:** Green

## Focus

Remember who you are! Transitions come and go on the journey. Change is inevitable. Yet, through it all we are to remember who we are and whose we are, also! As the leadership of Joshua comes to an end and the people transition from being nomads to settlers, it is essential that every tribe pledge allegiance to The Almighty. Joshua declares, "As for me and my house, we will serve the Lord." This is a ceremony of renewing the covenant made to Abram and Sarai generations ago. Five of the "virgins" forgot their role and function on the journey. When the cry to "go" was made, they were without the necessary equipment to light their way. They were called, "foolish." The covenant is renewed when Ruth gives birth to a child who is Obed, the grandfather of David, the great King. And, Jesus uses a poor widow's small offering as the model we are to use on the journey. 2 Thessalonians calls us to stand firm and hold onto the taught traditions. Remembering keeps us focused on who we are!

## Call to Worship

**Leader:** There is a word in the house this morning.
**People:** Are ears are on alert for what we will hear.
**Leader:** The truth of God as lived by our Ancestors will be rehersed.
**People:** The proverbs of Africa, the stories of yesteryear and the counsel of the elders will remind us
of who we are.
**Leader:** We will not keep the story to ourselves.
**People:** We want to refresh our minds and let our children hear as well.
**Leader:** The coming generations deserve to know our faith story.
**People:** We are on a journey. We pause to offer praise and worship as we go!

## Altar Focus

The Egyptian pyramids, writing tools, scientific discoverers, and African Kings and Queens help us to remember who we are! We need to make sure that those in our pews understand, realize and have internalized that our journey did not begin in the cotton fields, tobacco fields and plantations of the "home of the free and land of the slave!" There is another story that must be told. We cannot afford to wait for African American History Month. Every month is a month to uplift the history, the work ethics and the values of The Ancestors. Any individual of significance will help the entire congregation to remember their link to history. This is a good day to do a covenant renewal service for your membership. It's fall harvest time and budgets are being prepared and commitments will have to be made. Remind the people of who they are and to whom all belongs.

## MUSICAL SUGGESTIONS FOR THE TWENTY-SIXTH SUNDAY AFTER PENTECOST

### HYMNS FOR THE DAY

| Title | AAHH | AME | AMEZ | LEVS | LMGM | NNBH | TFBF | YL | HG |
|---|---|---|---|---|---|---|---|---|---|
| A Child of the King | 125 | 298 | 542 | • | • | 391 | • | 118 | • |
| All Creatures of Our God and King | 147 | 50 | 66 | • | • | 33 | • | 21 | • |
| Holy God, You Raised up Prophets | • | • | • | 46 | • | • | 299 | • | • |
| If Jesus Goes with Me | 555 | • | • | • | • | 443 | • | 497 | • |
| Lift Every Voice and Sing | 540 | 571 | • | 1 | 291 | 457 | 296 | 506 | • |
| The Battle Hymn of the Republic | 490 | 572 | • | 226 | 6 | 455 | 297 | 502 | • |

| Spirituals | AAHH | AME | AMEZ | LEVS | LMGM | NNBH | TFBF | YL | HG |
|---|---|---|---|---|---|---|---|---|---|
| He's Got the Whole World in His Hand | 150 | • | • | • | • | • | • | • | • |
| Siyahamba (We Are Marching) | 164 | • | • | • | • | • | 63 | • | • |
| Walk Together Children | 541 | • | • | • | • | • | • | • | • |
| We Are Climbing Jacob's Ladder | 464 | 363 | 603 | 220 | 54 | 217 | • | 363 | • |

| Gospel Selections | AAHH | AME | AMEZ | LEVS | LMGM | NNBH | TFBF | YL | HG |
|---|---|---|---|---|---|---|---|---|---|
| Close to Thee | 552 | 396 | • | 122 | • | 317 | • | • | • |
| I Don't Feel No Ways Tired | 414 | • | • | 199 | 159 | • | • | 364 | • |
| Precious Memories | 516 | • | • | • | • | 408 | • | • | • |
| Somebody Prayed for Me | 505 | • | • | • | • | • | 246 | • | • |

### ANTHEMS

Lift Every Voice and Sing   *arr. Roland M. Carter*

Song of Moses   *Robert Mayes*

The Torch Has Been Passed   *Lena McLin*

Nkosi Sikeleli Afrika

### GOSPEL SELECTIONS

Close to Thee   *arr. Dr. Robert E. Wooten*

When My House Became a Home   *V. Michael McKay*

### ORGAN MUSIC

Triumphal March of Heritage   *Uzee Brown, Jr.*

Go Down Moses   *Fela Sowande*

Joshua Fit de Battle ob Jericho   *Fela Sowande*

Prayer (Oba a ba ke)   *Fela Sowande*

# Twenty-Seventh Sunday after Pentecost
## November 13-November 19

**Year A:** Judges 4: 1-7/ Psalm 123/ 1 Thessalonians 5: 1-1/ Matthew 25: 14-30
**Year B:** 1 Samuel 1: 4-20/ 1 Samuel 2: 1-10, (The Canticle of Hannah)/ Hebrews 10: 11-18, 19-25/ Mark 13: 1-8
**Year C:** Isaiah 65: 17-25/ Isaiah 12, (The Song of Thanksgiving)/ 2 Thessalonians 3: 6-13, Luke 21: 5-19
**Appropriate Banner and Altar Colors:** Green

## Focus

The journey demands our whole life. We cannot reserve any part for ourselves. God demands our all! With God there is no difference between the sacred and the secular. For God made everything. So, our "personal" lives belong to God and Deborah, a wife and mother was selected to become General in Chief of God's Army as the only woman we know who served Israel is a judge. She was called from her "secular place" and sent into battle to win a strategic war. Hannah, a childless wife, has found her "secular" life to be hell. For the second wife of her husband is fertile, scornful and mean. Hannah's prayer for deliverance is the first one recorded by a woman. God hears and answers her prayer and uses her firstborn son, Samuel, as Israel's first priest-prophet. These are those called, by God, from their ordinary walks of life and allowed to do extraordinary things that benefit all. The unworthy and the barren are used to bless God's Realm. Ain't this good news?

## Call to Confession

For too long we have felt unworthy due to standards developed by other mere humans. Our worry and concern have left us as barren people before a fruitful God. This is sin. It is our time to confess and to repent.

## Confession

Harvest Maker, we sit with crushed spirits and wounded hearts. We have spent too much time trying to live up to the expectations of others, until we have not fully explored the destiny you have for us. We have allowed ourselves to be caught up in the syndrome of "contrast and compare." We have felt that we did not measure up, so we hesitated to make new attempts for your realm. We have sinned. We have fallen short of your glory. Forgive us, we pray in the name of The Righteous Vine.

## Altar Focus

This is an excellent Sunday to pay attention to the work of women who make homes in your local congregation. It's a good time to honor the kitchen committee who has kept your church well fed! Women working together; women tending children, women and men bringing children to church and a woman before a sink or stove speaks to the many places we may be when God calls us to go! Compare and contrast the prayer of Hannah with that of Mary's Magnificat. The power of prayer is an excellent focus to review for The Body of Christ.

# MUSICAL SUGGESTIONS FOR THE TWENTY-SEVENTH SUNDAY AFTER PENTECOST

## HYMNS FOR THE DAY

| Title | AAHH | AME | AMEZ | LEVS | LMGM | NNBH | TFBF | YL | HG |
|-------|------|-----|------|------|------|------|------|-----|-----|
| Here from All Nations | • | • | • | • | • | • | • | • | 46 |
| I'm Going Through, Jesus | • | • | • | • | • | 399 | • | • | • |
| If Jesus Goes with Me | 555 | • | • | • | • | 443 | • | 497 | • |
| Make Me a Blessing | • | • | • | 158 | • | 437 | • | 356 | • |
| Rescue the Perishing | • | 211 | 669 | • | • | 414 | • | 492 | • |
| Set My Soul Afire | • | • | • | • | • | 421 | • | • | • |
| To Worship, Work and Witness | • | • | • | • | • | 423 | • | • | • |

| Spirituals | AAHH | AME | AMEZ | LEVS | LMGM | NNBH | TFBF | YL | HG |
|-----------|------|-----|------|------|------|------|------|-----|-----|
| Ain't-a that Good News | • | • | • | 180 | • | • | • | 171 | • |
| I Will Trust in the Lord | 391 | ' | 75 | 193 | 232 | 285 | 256 | 333 | • |
| On My Journey Home | • | • | • | ' | • | 504 | • | • | • |

| Gospel Selections | AAHH | AME | AMEZ | LEVS | LMGM | NNBH | TFBF | YL | HG |
|-------------------|------|-----|------|------|------|------|------|-----|-----|
| The Broken Vessel | • | • | • | • | • | 535 | • | • | • |

## ANTHEMS

Create in Me a Clean Heart   *Paul Christiansen*

Thou Knowest, Lord, the Secrets of Our Hearts   *Henry Purcell*

Judge Eternal   *Gerre Hancock*

Be Followers of God   *Leo Sowerby*

## SPIRITUALS

Ain't-a that Good News   *arr. William Dawson*

Ain't-a that Good News   *arr. Moses Hogan*

I Will Trust in the Lord   *arr. Undine Smith Moore*

## GOSPEL SELECTIONS

Healing   *Richard Smallwood*

The Potter's House   *V. Michael McKay*

(See Appendix of Resources)

## ORGAN MUSIC

Fantasy and Fugue on "My Lord, What a Mourning"   *Ralph Simpson*

O God, Thou Faithful God   *Johannes Brahms*

Have Mercy on Me, O God, BWV 721   *J. S. Bach*

Jacob's Ladder   *Ralph Simpson*

# TWENTY-EIGHTH SUNDAY AFTER PENTECOST
## NOVEMBER 20-NOVEMBER 26
### CHRIST THE KING SUNDAY

**Year A:** Ezekiel 34: 11-16, 20-24/ Psalm 100/ Ephesians 1: 15-23/ Matthew 25: 31-46

**Year B:** 2 Samuel 23: 1-7/ Psalm 132: 1-18/ Revelation 1: 4b-8/ John 18: 33-37

**Year C:** Jeremiah 23: 1-6/ Luke 1: 68-79 (The Benedictus )/ Colossians 1:11-20/ Luke 23: 33-43

**Appropriate Banner and Altar Colors:** White or Gold

## FOCUS

Jesus deals with the end times. Jesus gives us a portrait of the eschatology that mystifies us. Jesus speaks to that which is to come when all of our going culminates before God's Throne. Jesus uses the image of separating sheep from goats, or the righteous from the unrighteous. Jesus has this affinity for little dumb looking, clannish sheep, for he names himself The Good Shepherd, who lays down his life for the sheep.

Those who have fed the hungry, given water to the thirsty, welcomed strangers, put clothes on the naked, visited the sick and imprisoned are put on the "right" side. Those who have used their days of going to ignore the "little sheep" are left out of The End of God's story with humans in the Church. What is odd, is that the righteous never knew that they were ministering unto The King! They only saw needs. And, in Love they responded as able. It was not about church offices, political legislation, fame, fortune and position after all. It was all about Love!

## CALL TO WORSHIP

**Leader:** The Good Shepherd is here to rescue every lost and straying sheep.

**People:** We, like sheep have all gone astray.

**Leader:** The One greater than David, sits on The Throne.

**People:** We are the sheep of his pasture. Our souls hunger and thirst for righteousness.

**Leader:** Come all that love the King of Kings and let your joy be well known!

**People:** Blessing, honor, glory and thanksgiving we bring as our sacrifice of praise. Worthy is the Lamb that was slain. We come to worship Christ the King.

## ALTAR FOCUS

The closing scene in *Coming to America* is an excellent clip to play as a prelude to worship if you are able. For it shows a multitude of royal people who are assembled with their best dress, awaiting the arrival of the guest of honor. In our nation, we have played down the role of our President and elected leaders. However, we need to be reminded, in as vivid a manner as possible, that the King reigns. There is no election except our vote to give him our pledge of allegiance with our lives! "Oh, I want to be there, to look upon his face!"

## MUSICAL SUGGESTIONS FOR THE TWENTY-EIGHTH SUNDAY AFTER PENTECOST

### HYMNS FOR THE DAY

| Title | AAHH | AME | AMEZ | LEVS | LMGM | NNBH | TFBF | YL | HG |
|---|---|---|---|---|---|---|---|---|---|
| All Creatures of Our God and King | 147 | 50 | 66 | · | · | 33 | · | 21 | 46 |
| Come, Thou (Now) Almighty King | 327 | 7 | 2 | · | 76 | 38 | · | 16 | · |
| O Worship the King | · | 12 | 4 | · | · | 6 | · | 3 | · |
| Rejoice, the Lord Is King (CHRIST CHURCH) | · | · | 197 | · | · | · | · | · | · |
| Rejoice, the Lord Is King (DARWALL'S 148TH) | · | 88 | · | · | 93 | · | · | 13 | · |
| Rejoice, the Lord Is King (LISCHER) | · | 89 | · | · | · | · | · | · | · |

| Spirituals | AAHH | AME | AMEZ | LEVS | LMGM | NNBH | TFBF | YL | HG |
|---|---|---|---|---|---|---|---|---|---|
| All Hail, King Jesus | 227 | · | · | · | · | 546 | · | · | · |
| Ride On, King Jesus | 225 | · | · | 97 | · | · | 182 | · | · |

| Gospel Selections | AAHH | AME | AMEZ | LEVS | LMGM | NNBH | TFBF | YL | HG |
|---|---|---|---|---|---|---|---|---|---|
| Perfect Praise | 296 | · | · | · | · | · | · | · | · |

### ANTHEMS

King of Glory, King of Peace   *Eric Thiman* or *Harold Friedell*

The Lord Shall Reign (2-pt)   *David Hurd*

Jesus Shall Reign   *Kimball/Van Camp*

Christ Is the King   "Christus Rex"/ *S. D. Wolf*

### SPIRITUALS

Ain't Got Time to Die   *Hall Johnson*

Ride On, King Jesus   *arr. Roland Carter*

Ride On, King Jesus   *arr. Moses Hogan*

### GOSPEL SELECTIONS

We Shall Behold Him   *Dottie Rambo/ arr. Larry Mayfield*

Worthy Is the Lamb   *Lamont Lenox* (GIA)

(See Appendix of Resources)

### ORGAN MUSIC

For He is King of Kings!   William F. Smith (*Songs of Deliverance*)

Partita on "Darwall's 148th"   *Charles Callahan*

Darwall's 148th.   *Joyce Jones*

Crown Him with Many Crowns   *Michael Burkhart*

# THANKSGIVING DAY

**Year A:** Deuteronomy 8: 7-18/ Psalm 65/ 2 Corinthians 9: 6-15/ Luke 17; 11-19
**Year B:** Joel 2: 21-27/ Psalm 126/ 1 Timothy 2: 1-7/ Matthew 6: 25-33
**Year C:** Deuteronomy 26: 1-11/ Psalm 100/ Philippians 4: 4-9/ John 6: 25-35
**Appropriate Banner and Altar Colors:** White or Gold

## FOCUS

Seek first the Realm of God and everything else is provided. So, we gather as thankful people to offer praise for the generousity of God. This Covenant Keeper has been faithful down through the generations and for this we celebrate and give freely of our appreciation. The children of Israel ran out of food and water. God provided all they ever needed! Can you imagine clothes that did not wear out; sandals that did not fall apart; the bread of angels and water from a rock in the midst of the desert! Mighty God! The Pilgrims were forced to put five grains of corn in each plate their second year in America. Their crops had failed and their rations had run out. But, due to the benevolence of God and the hunting skills of The Native Americans, they were fed and lived to tell about it. Have you ever wondered why it's only those of The African Dispora that make and eat sweet potato dishes? We brought them with us as we traveled The Middle Passage! God provided, even on slave ships! Come, thankful people and lift your voices in a concert of thanksgiving.

## CALL TO WORSHIP

**Leader:** How do we say "Thanks" to The Creator?
**People:** It is by our lives that we express true thanks unto God.
**Leader:** What does it mean to say much obliged to The Almighty?
**People:** We pause this day to recognize, honor and declare that without God, nothing exists.
**Leader:** When is the appropriate time to offer thanksgiving?
**People:** Every minute of every day is an appropriate time of giving thanks.
On this day, we gather to offer our collective worship to our faithful God.

## ALTAR FOCUS

The baking women should be called! The farmers and gardeners should be placed on notice! For as God provides another fall harvest, the abundance of grains can be made in a giant cornucopia and filled with the articles others have grown. All can be shared in the fellowship time as people see that once again we have been blessed by a generous God!

# MUSICAL SUGGESTIONS FOR THANKSGIVING DAY

## HYMNS FOR THE DAY

| Title | AAHH | AME | AMEZ | LEVS | LMGM | NNBH | TFBF | YL | HG |
|---|---|---|---|---|---|---|---|---|---|
| Come, Ye Thankful People, Come | 194 | 574 | 243 | • | 205 | 327 | • | • | • |
| Count Your Blessings | 533 | • | 626 | • | • | 325 | 173 | 35 | • |
| For All the Blessings of the Year | • | 577 | 116 | • | • | • | • | • | • |
| For the Beauty of the Earth | • | 578 | 6 | • | • | 8 | • | 68 | • |
| Now Thank We All Our God | • | 573 | 22 | • | 208 | 330 | • | • | • |
| We Gather Together | 342 | 576 | 28 | • | 307 | 326 | • | 8 | • |

| Gospel Selections | AAHH | AME | AMEZ | LEVS | LMGM | NNBH | TFBF | YL | HG |
|---|---|---|---|---|---|---|---|---|---|
| Everyday Is Thanksgiving | • | • | • | • | • | 328 | • | • | • |
| I Am So Grateful | • | • | • | • | 207 | • | • | • | • |
| I Thank You, Jesus | 532 | • | • | • | • | • | • | • | • |
| I Will Bless Thee, O Lord | 530 | • | • | • | • | • | • | • | • |
| One More Day | 538 | • | • | • | • | 548 | • | • | • |
| We Bring the Sacrifice of Praise | 529 | • | • | • | • | • | • | • | • |

## ANTHEMS

Give Thanks to the Lord *Willis L. Barnett*

I Will Give Thanks Unto Thee, O Lord *G. Rossini*

It Is a Good Thing to Give Thanks *David Hurd*

Lord, We Give Thanks Unto Thee *Undine Smith Moore*

O Give Thanks Unto the Lord (No. 33 in *Yes, Lord!*) *Iris Stevenson*

## SPIRITUALS

I Want to Thank You, Lord *Moses Hogan/arr. Benjamin Harlan*

## GOSPEL SELECTIONS

For Every Mountain *Kurt Carr*

Thank You *Richard Smallwood*

## ORGAN MUSIC

Festive Processional on "Now Thank We All Our God" *Michael Burkhardt*

Now Thank We All Our God *Sigfried Karg-Elert*

Postlude on OLD HUNDREDTH *Fred Bock*

Psalm of Praise (Toccata on OLD HUNDREDTH) *Charles Callahan*

Thanksgiving Suite *Charles Callahan*

We Thank Thee, God (Sinfonia to *Cantata No. 29*) *J.S. Bach/arr. Robert Hebble*

# THREE SPECIAL SERVICES

# THE YAM CEREMONY
## A Celebration for the Black Church

Joel 2: 21-27/Psalm 126/ 1 Timothy 2: 1-7/ Matthew 6: 25-33
Colors: Harvest Colors with Gold

## Call To Worship

Leader: Today we gather to celebrate the gift we are as African-Americans.

People: We celebrate our African roots.
We celebrate our spirituality, brought with us to these shores.
We celebrate our different ways of being that we share with the wider Church.
We celebrate the High God who has traveled with us all of our days.

Leader: Today we gather to celebrate the gift we are as African-Americans .

People: We affirm that we are on a journey, often from can to can't.
We affirm that STONY IS THE ROAD WE TROD, with the stumbling blocks of racism
often blocking our way.
We affirm that God has been our help in ages past and is our hope for the years to come.

Leader: Today we gather to celebrate the gift we are as African-Americans .

People: We have a song to sing. We have a story to tell.
We have our heroes and heroines to recall.
We have our own faith journey to share and our own rituals to rehearse.
We have a God to praise: we have a Christ to uplift and we have the Holy Spirit to magnify.

Unison: TODAY WE GATHER TO CELEBRATE THE GIFT WE ARE AS AFRICAN-AMERICANS.

Hymn of Praise "Lift Every Voice and Sing"

## Call to Confession

Now is the acceptable time. Today is the day of salvation. With open hearts and repentant spirits, let us turn, in confession, to the Ultimate One, who longs to be in Covenant relationship with us. Let us pray.

## Confession

Loving God, we are an unfaithful people. You created us in your image and breathed into us the breath of life. We have marred your image and done deeds of death to ourselves and to others. Have mercy on us. Blot out our sin and forgive us. Purge us and we will be clean. Wash us and we will be as pure as new fallen snow. Grant us a new and a right spirit we pray. Amen. (Adapted from *United Methodist Book of Worship* )

## Words of Assurance

Jesus Christ is the source of our forgiveness. He died for our sins once and for all to put to death the bonds which hold us. We are reconciled to God through Christ and made equal partners in the Covenant. God is merciful and compassionate, more ready to forgive than we are to ask. Rejoice and walk in the newness of life. Amen.

## JOYS AND CONCERNS OF THE COMMUNITY

Prayers of the People

**Leader:** "The yam is a life sustaining symbol of African American kinship and community. Everywhere in the world where we live, we grow, cook and eat yams. It is a symbol of our Diasporic connections. Yams provide nourishment for the body as food and are used medicinally to heal the body."[1] Today, as we gather to celebrate who we are as African-Americans in the Universal Church, may the symbol of the yam remind us of our strong roots, our hearty constitution, our necessity to the world and our spiritual connection to sisters and brothers everywhere. The yam was the food of our Ancestors, may we remember and honor their presence in us today. The yam is food for us. Let us give thanks for the plant of the ground which draws us together. The yam is our symbol of hope for our future generations. May we always remember our heritage as African-American Christians, with pride.

**Leader:** What symbol do you bring?

*The people bring their yams, baked sweet potatoes, yam breads, pies, cookies, soups, etc. forward to the altar for blessing.*

**Leader:** "What is wrong, old wife? What is happening to the people of the yam? Seem like they just don't know how to draw up the powers from the deep like before!"[2]

**People:** God of the yam, Creator of all things, we pause to give you thanks for the rich soil which produced our foreparents and was our homeland. The yam reminds us that you made us tough and durable, sweet and plentiful, resilient and tender. In your Divine Wisdom, you have nourished us and provided us with growth opportunities in all the places of the Diaspora. Our roots have held secure. Our knowledge has increased. Our community has been saved in spite of dangers, seen and unseen. Like the yam, we have grown in the deepness of your love. We have sprung forth in the proper time and become a bumper crop, willing to share our joy of abundant life. We call upon your power today.

**Leader:** Too often we have forgotten and neglected the power we have received from you. Too often we have believed that we were ugly and misshapen, as the yam. Many times we have despaired at our colors, as varied as the yam. And, we have been misused and neglected because of our durability, like the yam. Yet, the yam has endured the rigors of time and the storm-tossed travel, from shore to shore. And, it reminds us of our story and we call upon your power today.

**People:** We bless you for the yam and the many ways it has sustained us. As a protein staple it has fed us. As a tasty side-dish, it has been offered with our leafy greens. And, we have delighted in sweet potato pies and breads, which is our ethnic offering to the world. You have blessed us, a misused and neglected people, to be living symbols of your sustaining grace and care.

**Leader:** We call upon your powers today, Holy One. For the Black Church, its founders, who uplifted our uniqueness to the wider Church, and made us more aware of our sweet, sweet spirit of celebration and joy which needed to be spread. We call upon your powers.

**People:** Majestic Sovereign, we call upon your powers. For the Black Church everywhere, its leadership and direction, as we continue to walk a lonesome valley, and cry out for justice and long denied liberty, we pray.

**Leader:** Lavishly Generous God, we call upon your powers. For the people of the yam everywhere, we lift our hearts in prayer. As we gather to rehearse our faith story and to celebrate our witness to the wider world, we need your power in order that the Black Church might continue to be articulated courage, visible dignity, strong endurance and steadfast faithfulness in our service to you.

**People:** Name Above All Names, we offer thanksgiving for the ability to eat from the table which is loaded with symbols of our heritage. We bless you for knowing us and calling us by name. We bless you for the power we have from you to be valiant, strong, gentle and grace-filled as we face the days ahead. We bless you for the yam. We are thankful for food from home which has been a constant in our unsteady existence. However, because you have sustained the yam, we are assured that your grace will keep us and the Black Church in the generations ahead.

**Unison:** We are proud African-Americans, people of the yam. We will walk and talk with the power of God and give praise to the awesome high God always. Amen.

## HYMN OF PRAISE

"Let All the People Praise Thee" (#58 AME, #83 LMGM, #11 NNBH, #14 YL)

## SCRIPTURE LESSONS

## THE LIVING WORD

## HYMN OF RESPONSE

"Remember Me" (#434 AAHH, #179 LEVS, #209 LMGM)

## THE INVITATION TO OFFERING

People of the Yam know what is right. We are required to love justice, to seek mercy and to walk humbly with our God. People of the Yam do what is right. We share from our resources in order that all the community might prosper. People of the Yam give generously from hearts filled with thanks.

## THE OFFERTORY PRAISE

Yam maker and preserver, we are they who have acquired and mastered the art of stretch and make do! We appreciate your creative powers at work in us today. Receive these, our offerings, and multiply them for greater use in the world.

## THE DOXOLOGY

## THE BENEDICTION

**Leader:** You are African-Americans, people of the yam, made of beautiful black, rich earth.
**People:** We are African-Americans, people of the yam, brought by God to be a witness and lights in the world.
**Leader:** You are African-Americans, people of the yam, a gift to the Church and sacred to our God.
**People:** We are African-Americans, people of the yam, and we will continue to offer who we are,
for we are forever held in the loving arms of our God. Amen and Amen.

## Hymn of Benediction

"We Shall Overcome" (#542 AAHH, #640 AMEZ, #227 LEVS, #297 LMGM, #501 NNBH, #213 TFBF)

## Postlude

Triumphal March of Heritage    *Uzee Brown, Jr.*

## Notes:

This worship service has been adapted here for use by any African-American Congregation. It can be used as a Thanksgiving worship. or it may be used in February for Black History Month. Congregations need to announce early in the month that this worship has a heavy emphasis on sweet potatoes. Members should be asked to bring as many pies, cakes, muffins, and cookies, which can be blessed and then shared during the coffee hour. The worship committee should be encouraged to build an altar display featuring many different sizes and shapes of yams to be a focus for the day. Members will be asked to bring their contributions forth before the litany, in order that the congregation can see the many and varied items which yams can provide.

(Inspiration for this service was provided by Ms. Deborah Tinsley Taylor, a poet-singer-minister-sister friend, from Aurora, Illinois)

1., 2. From *Sisters of the Yam*, by Bell Hooks.

# A COMMUNION LITURGY

This entire service is an adaptation of the Communion Liturgies of the United Methodist Church's *Book of Worship* and is used with generous interpretation.

## CALL TO WORSHIP

**Leader:** Sisters and brothers, everything has been made ready. The table is spread!

**People:** We come to meet the Living God, who is beyond our intellectual comprehension
and is yet as close as our breath.

**Leader:** Everything has been made ready. The table is spread!

**People:** We gather to celebrate the Risen Christ, who is God with us and nevertheless, the One to Come.

**Leader:** Everything has been made ready! The table is spread!

**People:** We assemble to be revived by the life-renewing Holy Spirit, who empowers our search
for Shalom in this unfriendly world.

**Leader:** In the bread and in the wine we will receive strength for the journey.

**People:** Everything has been made ready. The table is spread! Thanks be to the Risen Christ. Amen.

## HYMN OF CELEBRATION

"All Hail the Power"

(CORONATION: #4 AME, #32 AMEZ, #88 LMGM, #3 NNBH, #10 YL)

(DIADEM: #293 AAHH, #5 AME, #33 AMEZ, #89 LMGM, #5 NNBH, #267 TFBF)

## CALL TO CONFESSION

When we gather to praise God, we remember that we are God's people who have preferred our wills to God's. Accepting God's power to become new persons in Christ, let us confess our sin before God and one another.

## CONFESSION

Eternal God, we confess that often we have failed to be an obedient Church. We have not done your will. We have broken your laws. We have rebelled against your love. We have not loved our neighbors. We have not heard the cry of the needy. Forgive us, we pray. Free us for joyful obedience through Jesus Christ, our Lord. Amen.

## SILENT CONFESSION

## WORDS OF ASSURANCE

**Leader:** Hear the Good News! "Christ died for us while we were yet sinners; that is God's own proof
of universal love toward us." In the Name of Jesus Christ you are forgiven.

**People:** In the name of Jesus Christ, we are forgiven! Glory to God. Amen.

## PRAYERS FOR THE COMMUNITY

Adapted from *Bread of Tomorrow/Prayers for Church Year*, Orbis Press
"Asian Women Doing Theology," p. 60-61

Response to each stanza: KUM BA YAH, MY LORD

**Leader:** Someone's crying today, Lord. And the cries are of millions. Hear the crying men and women, boys and girls. Capture the tears of fear and the suffering; the tears of weakness and pain; the tears of brokenness and disappointment. We are crying Lord. Transform our lives.

Response

**Leader:** Too many are dying today, Lord. Too many die of hunger and homelessness. Too many die because of the systemic racist structures which deny the poor and enhance the rich. Too many are dying, Lord, because we neglect the power and gifts you have placed within us and told us to utilize. Too many are dying because we are not fully united in purpose and determined to stand together and be your witnesses. Too many are dying, Lord. Transform our lives.

Response

**Leader:** Someone's praying today Lord, even while we wait. And, we join with the faithful at prayer, even with our feeble and weak voices; in our broken and halting speech; in our wrestling and struggling, trying to believe that you hear and answer our prayers. But, we are the someones today, Lord, while we wait in hope. We pray you will rekindle our spirits, touch us with your love and empower us for the journey. We are praying Lord. Transform our lives.

Response

**Leader:** For the healing of the nations, come by here, Lord. For the Balm in Gilead that is needed for our wounded bodies and grieving spirits, come by here. For the restoration of our families, the authentic coming together of our communities and for the salvation of our souls, come by here. For your Church, fractured and splintered, come by here. For your world, divided and in chaos, come by here. For the sake of the leaders you have placed over us and for the sake of Jesus Christ, Oh, Lord, come by here.

**People:** Amen and Amen.

## AFFIRMATION OF FAITH

We believe in the God of colors:
A creating God who formed us from the dust of black earth.
We believe that this God came in the form of a despised minority, named Jesus. He was born of a virgin,
   powerless, helpless and dependent. He was despised and rejected and carried our shame.
Without cause they hung him high, stretched him wide and mocked him as he died.
He died, at the hands of a lynch mob, for our sake.
Evil did not gain the victory, for Jesus rose, victorious over sin, death and hell.
We celebrate the risen Savior who gave his life for justice and equality of all.
We join his struggle as disciples. He has come and he will come again.

He knows our troubles and journeys in us, day by day. We affirm our counselor, the Holy Spirit, who is the wisdom of God.

Jesus Christ is our rock and our salvation, the ancient of days and the lion of the tribe.

Amen.

## THE HEBREW LESSON

## THE GOSPEL LESSON

## HYMN OF PREPARATION

In Me (#452 AAHH) *or* Is There a Word from the Lord?   *Glenn Burleigh*

## THE CHALLENGE OF THE WORD

## HYMN OF RESPONSE

The Decision (#388 AAHH)

## THE PEACE

The table is open to all who will receive the ministry of reconciliation and pass it on. Let's offer each other signs and symbols of God's Shalom.

# A SERVICE OF COMMUNION

## THE GREAT THANKSGIVING

Leader: The Lord is with you.

People: And also with you.

Leader: Lift up your hearts.

People: We lift them up to the Lord.

Leader: God of our Ancestors, hope of the living ones, we offer you praise and thanksgiving because you loved us enough to empty yourself of awesome Divinity and entered into our human struggle, taking upon yourself our despised color and position in life.

You have walked our valley of sorrow and felt the whip tear the flesh from your back.

You know what it means to be denied justice, and to be abandoned by friends.

So, when our nationality is reviled, our color scorned and our dignity defamed until we are without comfort or hope, we remember you.

You called together twelve and worked to achieve unity.

You taught self-determination and role-modeled hard work and responsibility.

You healed and set free in order that others might maintain their economic development and have purpose in their daily lives.

You are the essence of creativity and promised that greater works we would perform.

It was your faith that allowed you to march with determination up Golgatha's Hill.

With help from one Black Brother, Simon, you carried a cruel cross.

And, on that old, rugged cross you became our sin and shame, sanctifying pain and giving birth to the Universal Church.

So, with all the company of Saints, those who have walked with you to Calvary, that they might be raised to new life with you, we praise you, saying

**People:** Holy, Holy, Holy,

Compassionate, identifying God.

Heaven and earth are full of your glory;

Hosanna in the highest.

Blessed is the one

Who comes in the name of God;

Hosanna in the highest.

**Leader:** Blessed is our Savior, Jesus.

Bone of our bone and flesh of our flesh, who the cup of suffering did not shirk;

who, on the night that he was betrayed, took bread, gave thanks, broke it and said,

"This is my body, broken for you. Eat it, in remembrance of me."

In the same manner, after the supper, he took the cup, gave thanks and said:

"This cup is the new covenant in my blood.

It is poured out for you and for many, for theforgiveness of sin.

Whenever you drink it, remember me."

**People:** Christ has died.

Christ is risen.

Christ will come again.

**Leader:** As we eat this bread and drink this cup, we proclaim Christ's suffering and death until he comes. In the body that is broken and the cup that is poured out we restore to memory and hope, all of the unnamed and forgotten victims of blatant sins.

We hunger for the bread of that new age and thirst for the wine of the realm which is to come.

Come, Holy Spirit, hover over and dwell within these earthly things, and make us one body with Christ, that we, who are baptized into his death, may walk in newness of life; that what is sown in dishonor may be raised in glory, and what is sown in weakness may be raised in power.

**People:** Amen.

**Leader:** Sisters and Brothers, Christ has made everything ready. Come and eat, the table is spread.

## THE BREAKING OF THE BREAD

Lonely stalks of wheat, stood useless in a field, until they were pulled together, bruised, crushed, beaten and baked to become bread for a hungry world. When we break this loaf, it is our sharing in the Body of Christ.

## Taking of the Cup

Single grapes, lay close to the ground, until they were picked, stomped, crushed and smashed to provide drink for a thirsty world. When we give thanks over the cup, it is our sharing in the blood of Christ.

This is an open altar. All who name Jesus as Lord, to the glory of God, are welcome at this table.

## Doxology

## Benediction

**Leader:** We have gathered for community worship and feasting. Now we are sent again into the world, with the authority and power of the Holy Spirit.

**People:** The Lord has prepared a table for us, in the presence of our enemies.

**Leader:** We require nothing else for the journey. All our needs are supplied by an All Sufficient God.

**People:** A mighty fortress is our God, a shelter in time of storm.

**Leader:** The world has not changed. Evil continues. But, we are mandated by El Shaddai to make a difference.

**People:** We will cry loud and spare not!

We will lift up our voices like trumpets in Zion!

We will proclaim that this is the day of our God.

Amen and Amen.

## Hymn of Benediction

"My Tribute" (#111 AAHH, #610 AMEZ, #329 NNBH, #272 TFBF, #18 YL)

# A Worship of Death and New Life
## A Funeral Service

During the time of gathering, if there is not an organist present, there are many instrumental CDs that will provide soft background songs of faith. If there are musicians available, the following preludes would be appropriate:

All Humankind Must Perish, BWV 643   *J. S. Bach*

Adagio for Strings   *Samuel Barber*

Be Still, My Soul   *arr. Diane Bish*

Cortege et Litanie   *Marcel Dupre*

## LEADER:

In dying, Jesus destroyed death and hell. In rising from the dead, Jesus Christ won for all of us eternal life.

At God's time, the trumpet will sound and we shall be caught up to meet The King of Glory in the air. We have gathered to celebrate the life, death and new life of (*Name*).

Jesus said, "I am the resurrection and the life. Those who believe in me, even though they die, yet, shall they live, and whoever lives and believes in me shall never die. For, behold, I died and now am alive forevermore. I hold the keys of hell and death. Because I live, you shall also live." This is our faith. And, as (*Name*) was buried in a watery grave of baptism and professed Christ, we gather today, with both grief and with hope. We come to acknowledge our loss of a physical body for (*Name*), while we find comfort in the reality that resurrection is coming soon. Let's join our voices in a great hymn of our faith.

## HYMN  *(choose one)*

Come, Ye Disconsolate   (#421 AAHH)

O God, Our Help in Ages Past   (#170 AAHH)

O Thou, in Whose Presence   (#422 AAHH)

The Lord Is My Light   (#160 AAHH)

## INVOCATION

God, before there was a when or a where in this world, you had already designed the days of our lives. We thank you for being our Mighty God, our Redeemer and our Help. You long for relationship with us and breathed your spirit into us and allowed us to live. We gather today, giving you praise for the gift of (*Name*). This life was one that was fearfully and wonderfully made. This was truly one of your grand designs. We now have sad hearts because you have taken back your breath and we are left with an empty shell. You are Mystery. Death is mysterious. We don't know how to let go and to say farewell. So, we come to you in prayer.

We thank you for the balcony of saints now awaiting us on the other side of time. Thank you for their labor among us and for the faith that they claimed and passed on to us. We come asking for your comfort, strength and guidance as we face the long and dreary days before us.

Bless now this grieving family. Bless them with the wonderful gift of memory that recalls their loved one to mind. Let your grace and your peace be multiplied in and among them, that their lives will bear witness that (*Name*) made a great difference in their lives. Bless us, their extended family. Let this reunion be a time of sharing and celebrating your great love. Help us and allow this worship to begin the process of healing that only your Holy Spirit can provide. This we ask in the name of The One who is our eternal home.

**Anthem or Solo** *(choose one)*

There Is a Balm in Gilead   *arr. William Dawson*

The Souls of the Righteous   *Ralph Vaughan Williams*

We Shall Behold Him   (#583 AAHH)

How Lovely Is Thy Dwelling Place   *Johannes Brahms*

Psalm 46: God Is Our Refuge and Strength   *John Weaver*

## The Psalms

*(Read)* 130, or 139:7-18

Psalms 23 *May be recited as an unison prayer*

## Hebrew Scripture

Isaiah 40: 28-31, Job 14: 1-15

## Hymn of Response

Leave It There   (#420 AAHH)

## The Reading of Message text

## Hymn or Solo

Oh, To Be Kept by Jesus   (#423 AAHH)

All My Help Comes from the Lord (#370 AAHH)

## Sermon

## Tributes

*Here the obituary is read and flowers and memorials noted.*

## Witness

*Friends and family offer short words of memory and comfort*

## Hymn

Guide Me, O Thou Great Jehovah   (#140 AAHH)

My Faith Looks Up to Thee   (#456 AAHH)

## A Statement of our Faith

> We believe in God and the Only Begotten Son, Jesus Christ who was sent to live in our world, to walk in our shoes, and to role model abundant life for us.
>
> We believe in The Holy Spirit, active in the world and in us as power, keeper,
>
> Comforter, Counselor and guide.
>
> We believe in God's universal Church without walls.
>
> We believe in repentance of sin, the baptism of all believers, the transforming of our minds and life eternal.

Consequently, we are not foreigners and aliens, but citizens with God's people and members of God's household, built on the foundation of the apostles and prophets, with Christ Jesus as the chief cornerstone. In him the whole building is joined together and rises to become a holy temple in the Lord.

In Jesus Christ we too are being built together to become a dwelling in which God's Holy Spirit is at home. We have become servants of this gospel by the gift of God's grace. For this we are thankful. On these facts rest our faith.

## HYMN

The Solid Rock   (#385 AAHH)

## BENEDICTION

Now may the God of peace

Who brought back from the dead our Lord Jesus,

The great shepherd of the sheep, by the blood

Of the eternal covenant, make us complete in everything

Good so that we might do God's will, working that which is pleasing God

Through Jesus Christ to whom be the glory forever and ever. (Hebrews 13: 20-21)

## RECESSIONAL

When We All Get to Heaven   (#594 AAHH)

On Jordan's Stormy Banks   (#586 AAHH)

## APPROPRIATE POSTLUDES

Prelude on SINE NOMINE   *Ralph Vaughan Williams*

Fugue in Eb on ST. ANNE, BWV 552   *J. S. Bach*

Carillon de Westminster   *Louis Vierne*

God of Grace and God of Glory   *Paul Manz*

# A MUSIC WORSHIP WORKSHEET

Date: ————————————————————————————————————

Season of the Church Year: ————————————————————————

Hebrew Scripture: ————————————————————————————

Psalm: ——————————————————————————————————

Epistle: ——————————————————————————————————

Gospel Leader: ————————————————————————————————

1. What are the major images that rise from these readings? ————————————
——————————————————————————————————————
——————————————————————————————————————
——————————————————————————————————————

2. What is the major challenge in your life presently? ——————————————
——————————————————————————————————————
——————————————————————————————————————
——————————————————————————————————————

3. Personal Leader: ————————————————————————————
——————————————————————————————————————
——————————————————————————————————————
——————————————————————————————————————

4. Choir related: ——————————————————————————————
——————————————————————————————————————
——————————————————————————————————————
——————————————————————————————————————
——————————————————————————————————————

5. Congregational Leader: _____

_____

_____

_____

6. Social environment: _____

_____

_____

_____

7. What hope is offered to you from God's Word for Sunday?

_____

_____

_____

8. What music speaks to these scriptures for you? _____

_____

_____

_____

9. What does the Living Word invite the People of God to do?

_____

_____

_____

10. What anthems relay these passages? _____

_____

_____

_____

11. What are the major issues facing the people in scriptures?

_____

_____

_____

12. How are the issues relevant to your local congregation? _____

_____

_____

_____

13. What music speaks to these contemporary issues? _____

_____

_____

_____

14. What is surprising/unexpected to you in these passages? _____

_____

_____

_____

15. What is comforting to you? _____

_____

_____

_____

16. What is the music that will be a call to worship for this service? _____

_____

_____

_____

17. What gospel song touches these passages? _____

_____

_____

_____

18. What contemporary music addresses these scriptures? _____

_____

_____

_____

19. Is there a piece of music that the Praise Dance Team might consider? _____

_____

_____

_____

20. How does the altar, banners, and overhead assist the congregation with "getting" the message? _____

_____

_____

_____

21. How can you tie these scriptures in with the title of the pastor's message? _____

_____

_____

_____

Additional comments: _____

_____

_____

_____

_____

_____

_____

_____

_____

_____

_____

_____

_____

_____

_____

_____

_____

_____

# APPENDIX OF RESOURCES

## 1. The Mass of Saint Augustine

*A Gospel Mass for Congregation, SATB Choir, and Piano by Leon C. Roberts*

**Publisher:**

GIA Publications, Inc.

7404 South Mason Avenue, Chicago, IL 60638

Telephone: 1 800 442 1358 • FAX: 708 496 3828 • www.giamusic.com or custserv@giamusic.com

**Publisher Catalog Numbers:**

| | | | |
|---|---|---|---|
| G-2448 | Complete SATB Choral/Vocal Score | 564-F | Congregation Card |
| MS-160 | Stereo Recording | | |

**The Mass of St. Augustine/individual Octavo Editions:**

| | | | |
|---|---|---|---|
| G-2468 | Thank you, Lord (Opening Song) | G-2507 | Lord, Have Mercy (Kyrie) |
| G-2469 | Glory to God (Gloria) | G-2470 | Let Us Go Rejoicing |
| G-2471 | Alleluia | G-2472 | Eucharistic Prayer Acclamations |
| G-2473 | The Lord's Prayer | | (Sanctus, Memorial Acclamation |
| G-2474 | Lamb of God (Agnus Dei) | | and Doxology) |
| G-2475 | Remember Me | | |
| G-2476 | He Has the Power | | |

**General Comments:**

- Excellent, accessible way to introduce Mass setting
- Movements are relatively easy and short
- Frequent use of easy homophonic, "hymn-like" writing
- Effective relationship between dynamics and text
- Could be used with bass guitar and drum set on any or all movements
- Tenor reads in same treble clef (shared) as sopranos and altos at times
- Entire Mass offered as separate octavos from publisher

## 2. The Mass of Saint Martin de Porres

*A Gospel Mass for Congregation, SATB Choir, Soli, and Piano by Leon C. Roberts*

*(Orchestra Scores available from Publisher)

**Publisher:**

Oregon Catholic Press Publications

5536 Northeast Hassalo Street, Portland, Oregon 97213

1-800-LITURGY or 1-877-596-1653 • www.ocp.org or liturgy@ocp.org

**Publisher Catalog Numbers:**

| | |
|---|---|
| 10393 | Complete SATB Choral/Vocal Score |

**Professional Recordings Available from:**

GIA Publications, Inc.

7404 South Mason Avenue, Chicago, IL 60638

Telephone: 1 800 442 1358 • FAX: 708 496 3828 • www.giamusic.com or custserv@giamusic.com

CD-342 Compact Disc Recording • CS-342 Cassette Recording

**The Mass of St. Martin de Porres:**

| | |
|---|---|
| I Call Upon You, God! (Gathering Song) | Lord, Have Mercy (Kyrie) |
| Glory to God in the Highest (Gloria) | Taste and See the Goodness of the Lord |
| Alleluia (Gospel Acclamation) | (Responsorial Psalm) |
| General Intercessions | I Surrender All |
| Holy, Holy, Holy (Sanctus) | Keep In Mind (Memorial Acclamation) |
| Great Amen | The Lord's Prayer/Doxology |
| Lamb of God (Agnus Dei) | Jesus Is Here Right Now (Communion Hymn) |
| Mary's Canticle | His Eye Is On the Sparrow (Meditation Hymn), |
| Give Us Peace (Sending Forth) | arr. Jeffrey LaValley |

**Individual Octavo Editions Available from Oregon Catholic Press:**

| | | | |
|---|---|---|---|
| 10397 | Give Us Peace (Sending Forth) | 10398 | I Surrender All |
| 10399 | Jesus Is Here Right Now | 10400 | Taste and See the Goodness of the Lord |
| 10449 | His Eye is On the Sparrow, arr. Jeffrey LaValley | | |

**Individual Octavo Editions Available from GIA Publications, Inc.**

| | | | |
|---|---|---|---|
| G-4327 | I Call Upon You, God! | G-3826 | Mary's Canticle |

General Comments:

- Involves styles ranging from Gregorian chant to contemporary gospel
- Congregation parts are easy as to encourage participation
- Reflects on the universality of both Catholic and Protestant traditions
- Syncopated and filled with rhythmic energy
- Somewhat lengthy movements
- Almost 1/2 of this mass is available as separate octavos

# 3. The Mass of Saint Cyprian

*A Gospel Mass for Congregation, SATB Choir, Soli, and Piano by Kenneth W. Louis*

*(Orchestra Scores available from Publisher)

**Publisher:**

GIA Publications, Inc.

7404 South Mason Avenue, Chicago, IL 60638

Telephone: 1 800 442 1358 • FAX: 708 496 3828 • www.giamusic.com or custserv@giamusic.com

### Publisher Catalog Numbers:

| | | | |
|---|---|---|---|
| G-5173 | Complete SATB Choral/Vocal Score | 613-F | Assembly (Congregation) Edition |
| CD-462 | Compact Disc Recording | CS-462 | Cassette Recording |

### The Mass of St. Cyprian:

| | |
|---|---|
| The Procession: The Lord Will Hear the Just | Lord Have Mercy (Kyrie) |
| Glory To God (Gloria) | Responsorial Psalm: Proclaim God's Marvelous Deeds |
| Gospel Acclamation: Alleluia | Offertory: I'm Willing Lord |
| Preface Acclamation: Holy, Holy (Sanctus) | Memorial Acclamation: Dying you Destroyed |
| Great Amen | Our Death |
| Our Father (The Lord's Prayer) | Lamb of God (Agnus Dei) |
| Communion Hymn: Taste and See | Jesus, You Brought Me All the Way |

### Individual Octavo Editions:

| | | | |
|---|---|---|---|
| G-5637 | Communion Hymn: Taste and See | G-5142 | The Procession and Responsorial Psalm (The Lord Will Hear the Just/Proclaim God's Marvelous Deeds) |

### General Comments:

- Call and Response used throughout
- Rich, stately choral writing
- Almost entirely homophonic; some unison singing; not to rhythmically involved
- Movements are short; appropriate for worship service in separate parts or in small groups
- Varied styles, tempi, and key signatures
- Piano part accessible and lends itself to additional improvisation as musician or conductor sees fit

## 4. Alpha Mass, Opus 30

*A Gospel Mass for SATB Choir, Soli, and Piano by Glenn Burleigh*
*(Orchestra Scores available from Publisher)

### Publisher:

Glenn Burleigh Music Workshop and Ministry, Inc.

Post Office Box 16901, Oklahoma City, OK 73113

405 842 3470—Music Orders • 405 232 7477—Administrative Offices • wwwglenmusik.com or glenmusik@aol.com

### Publisher Catalog Numbers:

| | |
|---|---|
| Complete Choral/Vocal Score | Cassette Recording |
| Full Orchestral Score (Conductor's Edition) | Instrumental/Orchestral Parts |

### Alpha Mass:

| | |
|---|---|
| The Gathering | Create In Me A Clean Heart |
| Kyrie (Lord, Have Mercy) | Gloria (Gloria) |
| Matthew, Mark, Luke, And John | Alleluia |
| Credo (I Believe) | Sanctus (Holy) |

| | |
|---|---|
| Memorial Acclamation | Do This In Remembrance Of Me |
| For The Kingdom (The "Our Father") | Agnus Dei (Lamb of God) |
| Joy | There's A King On the Throne |
| Go In Peace | |

**Individual Octavo Editions Available from Publisher:**

Do This In Remembrance Of Me                Gloria

**General Comments:**

- English and Latin texts; Divided into four (4) section
- Classical, jazz, and gospel styles represented
- Medium-Difficult
- Movements tied together with textual theme of "Unity in the Kingdom" of God
- Able to actively include congregation in several areas
- Excellent performance suggestions and descriptions of each section provided by composer

# 5. Gospel Mass

*A Mass Setting for SATB Choir, Soli, and Piano by Robert Ray*
\*(Orchestra Scores available from Composer)

**Publisher:**

Jenson Publications/Hal Leonard Publications

7777 West Bluemound Road, Post Office Box 13819, Milwaukee, WI 53213 • 414 774 3630 • www.halleonard.com

\*Does not accept orders online

**Publisher Catalog Numbers:**

| | | | |
|---|---|---|---|
| HL44707014 | Complete SAT13 Choral/Vocal Score | HL08740901 | CID Recording |

**Gospel Mass:**

| | |
|---|---|
| KYRIE—Lord Have Mercy | GLORIA—Glory to God in the Highest |
| CREDO—I Believe in God | ACCLAMATION—Hallelujah Praise the Lord |
| SANCTUS—Holy, Holy Lord of Hosts | AGNUS DEI—Lamb of God |

**Individual Octavo Editions:**

| | | | |
|---|---|---|---|
| HL08595487 | CREDO—I Believe in God | HL08595483 | ACCLAMATION—Hallelujah Praise the Lord |

**Instrumental Accompaniment Recordings:**

| | | | |
|---|---|---|---|
| HL08740900 | Gospel Mass [SHOWTRAX CASSETTE] | HL08740901 | Gospel Mass [SHOWTRAX CD] |

**General Comments:**

- One of the most popular gospel settings of the Ordinary
- Nice integration of solo material within the choral writing
- Mostly homophonic, with use of divisi
- Nice for Easter/Lent or Christmas/Advent

- Careful attention to dynamic contrast in repeated sections
- Recently scored for orchestra
- Bass Guitar and Percussion parts included in SATB vocal score
- Improvisation encouraged for soloists and musicians

## 6. Lamentation and Celebration, Opus 43

*A Commissioned Work in Memory of the Oklahoma City Bombing of April 19, 1995, by Glenn Burleigh*

for SATB Choir, Brass Choir, Bass, Percussion/Timpani, Piano and Organ

*(Orchestra Scores available from Publisher)

Publisher:

Glenn Burleigh Music Workshop and Ministry, Inc.

Post Office Box 16901, Oklahoma City, OK 73113

405 842 3470—Music Orders • 405 232 7477—Administrative Offices • wwwglenmusik.com or glenmusik@aol.com

**Publisher Catalog Numbers:**

| | |
|---|---|
| Complete Choral/Vocal Score | [Item #GB1001-A] Cassette Recording |
| Full Score (Conductor's Edition) | Instrumental/Orchestral Parts |
| Orchestral Arrangement (coming soon!) | |

**Lamentation and Celebration:**

| | |
|---|---|
| Mercy | Happiness |
| Trouble | Deliverance |
| Joy | |

**Individual Octavo Editions Available from Publisher:** None

**General Comments:**

- Medium-Difficult, divisi writing
- Elements of gospel/jazz throughout; makes use of medieval chant-like passages; imitative fugue-like areas
- Uses tympani, organ pedals, and lower register of piano to dramatize tragedy; bomb blast is written in score as well as flashing red lights, sirens, and "screams in the crowd."
- Movements could be performed separately, but would work better together for dramatic impact
- Happiness—Excellent anthem for Sunday morning worship service
- Emotions of the piece re-enforced through rhythm and dynamics

# 7. The Coming

*A Celebration of Advent and Christmas for SATB Choir, Soli, Congregation, Piano, Organ, Percussion, Lead/Bass Guitar by Leon C. Roberts*
*(Orchestra Scores available from Publisher)

**Publisher:**

Oregon Catholic Press Publications

5536 Northeast Hassalo Street, Portland, Oregon 97213

1-800-LITURGY or 1-877-596-1653 • www.ocp.org or liturgy@ocp.org

**Publisher Catalog Numbers:**

| | | | |
|---|---|---|---|
| #10403 | Complete Choral/Vocal Score | #10404 | Cassette Recording |
| | *with instrumental parts | #10405 | Compact Disc Recording |
| | Full Orchestral Score (Conductor's Edition) | | |
| | Instrumental/Orchestral Parts | | |

**The Coming:**

| | |
|---|---|
| Come, Lord Jesus, Come! | Kyrie |
| Lord, Make Us Turn To You | Alleluia |
| Wait On The Lord | Holy, Holy, Holy *Audio Sample Available |
| Memorial Acclamation | At Publisher's Website |
| Great Amen | Lord's Prayer and Doxology |
| Lamb of God | We Remember You |
| He Shall Be Called Wonderful | |

**Individual Octavo Editions Available From Publisher:**

| | |
|---|---|
| #10591 | He Shall Be Called Wonderful |
| | *Audio Sample Available At Publisher's Website |
| #10783 | Lord Make Us Turn To You |
| #11045 | We Remember You |

**General Comments:**

- Use of modal chant style; accessible homophonic singing, flavored with gospel-styled rhythms; includes a "rap."
- Mass setting that calls for contemporary society to allow God to be born within each person
- Composer provides concise instructions for interpretation/style for even the novice musician
- Would be fitting for anytime of year

## 8. Born to Die, Opus 25

*A Christmas Cantata for SATB Choir, Soli, and Piano by Glenn Burleigh*

*(Orchestra Scores available from Publisher)

**Publisher:**

Glenn Burleigh Music Workshop and Ministry, Inc.

Post Office Box 16901, Oklahoma City, OK 73113

405 842 3470—Music Orders • 405 232 7477—Administrative Offices • wwwglenmusik.com or glenmusik@aol.com

**Publisher Catalog Numbers:**

| | |
|---|---|
| Complete Choral/Vocal Score | Cassette Tape Recording (2 tape set) |
| Full Orchestral Score (Conductor's Edition) | Instrumental/Orchestral Parts |

**Born To Die:**

| | |
|---|---|
| Born To Die | My Soul Doth Magnify The Lord (Song of Mary) |
| The Travail | Well, The Savior Is Born |
| Fear Not For Behold | What Shall I Render? (Song of the Wise Men) |
| Go Back Another Way | Why Do The Heathen Rage? (Song of Herod) |
| Mothers' Lament | Not 'Til I've Seen Jesus (Song of Simeon) |
| The Magnificat | You Shall Be Free Indeed |
| What's In A Name? | I Know That My Redeemer Liveth |
| With His Stripes We Are Healed | Keep-A Preachin' The Word |
| Born To Die (Reprise) | The Song Of The Lord |
| His Yoke Is Easy | Hosanna |

**Individual Octavo Editions Available from Publisher:**

| | |
|---|---|
| Born To Die | His Yoke Is Easy |
| My Soul Doth Magnify The Lord | Why Do the Heathen Rage? (Song of Herod) |
| Hosanna | Keep-A Preachin' The Word |
| The Magnificat | What's In a Name |

**General Comments:**

- Multiplicity of musical taste/styles
- Divided into two (2) sections, with scriptural references (narration)
- Rich choral passages that explore the vocal range
- Some challenging, imitative areas; frequent use of divisi
- Piano part is very technically involved; However, composer encourages improvisation throughout "freedom within structure"
- Excellent performance suggestions given by composer
- Could be performed as an oratorio or full-scale cantata (with drama, dance, and staging)

## 9. The Nguzo Saba Suite, Opus 41

*A Kwanzaa Celebration for SATB Choir, Soli, and Piano by Glenn Burleigh*
*(Orchestra Scores available from Publisher)

**Publisher:**

Glenn Burleigh Music Workshop and Ministry, Inc.

Post Office Box 16901, Oklahoma City, OK 73113

405 842 3470—Music Orders • 405 232 7477—Administrative Offices • wwwglenmusik.com or glenmusik@aol.com

**Publisher Catalog Numbers:**

| | |
|---|---|
| Complete Choral/Vocal Score | [item #GB1001-A] Cassette Recording |
| Full Orchestral Score (Conductor's Edition) | Instrumental/Orchestral Parts |

**The Nguzo Saba Suite, Opus 41:**

| | |
|---|---|
| Umoja (Unity) | Kujichagulia (Self-Determination) |
| Ujima (Collective Work and Responsibility) | Ujamma (Cooperative Economics) |
| Nia (Purpose) | Kuumba (Creativity) |
| Imani (Faith) Finale | |

**Individual Octavo Editions Available From Publisher:**

| | |
|---|---|
| Nia | Ujima |

**General Comments:**

- 30-35 minutes for entire work
- Medium-Difficult
- Movements 2-6 are strongly recommended by composer for church
- choir/worship
- Movements 1 and 7 are concert-like in nature and somewhat involved
- Chant-like in some areas; lyrical unison sections; interesting treatment of intervals (with descending fourths and parallel chordal movement)
- Dramatic use of dynamics
- Nia and Ujamma highly recommended for youth choirs

## 10. Let God Arise

*An Easter Cantata for SATB Choir, Soli, and Piano by Glenn Burleigh*
*(Orchestra Scores available from Publisher)

**Publisher:**

Glenn Burleigh Music Workshop and Ministry, Inc.

Post Office Box 16901, Oklahoma City, OK 73113

405 842 3470—Music Orders • 405 232 7477—Administrative Offices • wwwglenmusik.com or glenmusik@aol.com

**Publisher Catalog Numbers:**

Complete Choral/Vocal Score

Compact Disc Recording (2 CD Set)

Full Orchestral Score (Conductor's Edition)

Instrumental/Orchestral Parts

Excerpts/9 Songs (Cassette)

**Let God Arise**

Anoint Us

O For A Thousand Tongues To Sing

Prepare Me A Body (TTBB)

Follow Mc

Hosanna, Hosanna

Song Of the Disciples

Do This In Remembrance Of Me

Give Us Barabbas/I Find No Fault

When Thou Comest

See How They Done My Lord

I'm Gonna 'Rise

Faithful Over A Few Things

You Must Be Born Again

You Must Be Like A Child

Jesus Is

What Does All This Mean?

I'm Gonna Rise (Reprise)

Hallelujah, Hosanna (Reprise)

When Jesus 'Rose

My Good Lord Done Been Here

Let the Redeemed Say So

Let God Arise

# WOW Gospel Songbook Collections
are available through 'N' Time Music by contacting Sales Support Staff at 704-531-8961
or via e-mail at: info@ntimemusic.com

## WOW GOSPEL 1998 includes arrangements of the following:

| | |
|---|---|
| Be Encouraged | Beyond The Veil |
| Crucified With Christ | Every Time |
| Glad I've Got Jesus | Glory to Glory to Glory |
| God Cares | Gotta Feelin' |
| Greatest Part of Me | He's An On Time God |
| Heaven | Holy is the Lamb |
| I've Got a Testimony | Jesus is My Help |
| Jesus Paid It All | No Weapon |
| Not the Time, Not the Place | Order My Steps |
| Shout | Speak to My Heart |
| Stand (John P. Kee) | Stir Up '98 |
| Stomp | Stranger |
| Thank You, Lord | The Battle's the Lord's |
| The Call | Total Praise |
| We'll Understand It Better By and By | You Don't Have to Be Afraid |

## WOW GOSPEL 1999 includes arrangements of the following:

| | |
|---|---|
| Angel's Watching Over Me | Balm in Gilead |
| Clean Up | Don't Give Up on Jesus |
| Follow Me | For Every Mountain |
| Give It Up | Hold On |
| I Believe | I Will Bless the Lord |
| I Will Love You | I'm Too Close |
| If It Had Not Been for the Lord On My Side | In Harm's Way |
| Jesus, I Won't Forget | Just a Little Talk With Jesus |
| Just as Soon | Let the Praise Begin |
| Long As I Got King Jesus | Need to Know |
| Only Believe | So Good |
| Stand Up On Your Feet | Strength |
| Testify | The Vision |
| Under the Influence | Well Alright |
| What a Friend | When Will We Sing the Same Song |
| Worship Christ | You're Next in Line for a Miracle |
| You're the One | |

## WOW GOSPEL 2000 includes arrangements of the following:

Awesome God

Give Thanks

Goodtime

Healing

I Know the Lord

I'd Rather Have Jesus

It's All About Love

Lighthouse

Never Seen the Righteous

Oh, What a Friend

Put Your War Clothes On

Revive Us

Secret Place

Testify

We Worship You

Word Iz Bond

Caravan of Love

God Can

Hark, The Herald Angels Sing

I Come to You More Than I Give

I Made It

In Your Will

Jesus is All

Mighty God

Oh Happy Day

Power Belongs to God

Real With U

Safe in His Arms

Strong Man

Unconditional Love

Who Do You Love

Wrapped Up

## WOW GOSPEL 2001 includes arrangements of the following:

Alabaster Box

Battlefield

Closer to You

Fall Down 2000

God's Favor

I Anoint Myself

I Want My Destiny (LIVE)

If It Had Not Been for the Lord On My Side

Let's Dance (Remix)

Memories (When Will I See You Again?)

Once

Real

Right Here

Still I Rise

That'll Do It

Walk Right

At the Table

Better Days

Everyday

God's Got It

His Love

I Came to Jesus

I'll Keep on Holding On

It's Alright (Send Me)

Mary, Don't You Weep

Nothing Else Matters

Personal Jesus

Rejoice

Shackles (Praise You)

Tell It

The Holy Place

We Fall Down

**WOW GOSPEL 2002 includes arrangements of the following:**

And Yet I'm Saved

Born Again

Dear Lord

Gotta Worship

I Believe (Live)

If We Faint Not

II Chronicles

Jesus Can Work It Out

Prayer Changes Things

Stand Up

The Battle

Unconditional

When I Think About You

Yolanda Adams

You Didn't Have To

Be Right

Calvary

Deeper

I Believe

I Want to Be Ready

If We Pray

It's All About You

King of Kings

Run to the Water

That's What I Believe

These Thorns

Victory (Live)

When My Season Comes

You Are the Living Word

**WOW GOSPEL 2003 includes arrangements of the following:**

A Secret Place

Anyhow

Can't Give Up Now

Do Your Will

Glad About It

God's Got a Blessing with Your Name on It

Heard a Word

I'll Make It

In the Sanctuary

King of Glory

Nobody

People Get Ready

Praying Women

Standing on the Rock

Takin' It to the Streets

The Best is Yet to Come

Without Him

Anthem of Praise

Beautiful

Closet Religion

Drug Me

God Has Not 4Got

He's the Greatest

I Need You Now

I'll Trust You, Lord

Jesus, Jesus, Jesus

Let Us Worship Him

One More Battle to Fight

Praise is What I Do

Send a Revival

Superman

That Ain't Nothing

There's Nobody Like Jesus

## Sources: Books

Abbington, James. *Let Mt. Zion Rejoice! Music in the African American Church.* Valley Forge, PA: Judson Press, 2001.

Abbington, James., ed. *Readings in African American Church Music and Worship.* Chicago: GIA Publications, 2001.

Abbington, James and Linda H. Hollies. *Waiting to Go! African American Church Worship Resources from Advent through Pentecost.* Chicago: GIA Publications, Inc., 2002.

Costen, Melva Wilson. *African American Christian Worship.* Nashville: Abingdon Press, 1993.

Dudley, Grenae D. and Carlyle F. Stewart III. *Sanfoka: Celebrations for the African-American Church.* Cleveland: United Church Press, 1997.

Garcia, William Burres. "Church Music by Black Composers: A Bibliography of Choral Music" in *Readings in African American Church Music and Worship.* Chicago: GIA Publications, 2001. pp 385–407.

Hayes, Diana L. *Were You There? Stations of the Cross.* Maryknoll, NY: Orbis Books, 2000.

Hollies, Linda H. *Trumpet in Zion: Worship Resources, Year A.* Cleveland: Pilgrim Press, 2001.

Hollies, Linda H. *Trumpet in Zion: Worship Resources, Year B.* Cleveland: The Pilgrim Press, 2002.

Hollies, Linda H. *Trumpet in Zion: Worship Resources, Year C.* Cleveland: The Pilgrim Press, 2003.

Kirk-Duggan, Cheryl A. *African American Special Days: 15 Complete Worship Services.* Nashville: Abingdon Press, 1996.

Laster, James. *Catalogue of Choral Music Arranged in Biblical Order.* Second Edition. Lanham, MD: Scarecrow Press, 1996.

Mapson, Wendell J., Jr. *The Ministry of Music in the Black Church.* Valley Forge, PA: Judson Press, 1984.

McClain. William B. *Come Sunday: The Liturgy of Zion.* Nashville: Abingdon Press, 1990.

Spencer, Donald A. *Hymn and Scripture Selection Guide: A Cross-Reference Tool for Worship Leaders.* Grand Rapids, MI: Baker Book House, 1993.

Spencer, Jon Michael. *Black Hymnody: A Hymnological History of the African-American Church.* Knoxville, TN: The University of Tennessee Press, 1992.

Talbot, Frederick H. *African American Worship: New Eyes for Seeing.* Lima, OH: Fairway Press, 1998.

Warren, Gwendolin Sims. *Ev'ry Time I Feel the Spirit: 101 Best-Loved Psalms, Gospel Hymns, and Spiritual Songs of the African-American Church.* New York: Henry Holt and Company, 1997.

White, Evelyn Davidson. *Choral Music by African American Composers: A Selected, Annotated Bibliography,* 2nd Edition. Lanham, MD: Scarecrow Press, 1996.

## Sources: Websites

| | |
|---|---|
| www/agohq.org | The American Guild of Organists |
| www.Choralnet.org | ChoralNet, USA |
| www.giamusic.com | GIA Publications, Inc., Chicago, IL |
| www.glennmusik.com | Glenn Burleigh Music Workshop and Music Ministry, Oklahoma City, OK |
| www.halleonard.com | Hal Leonard Publications, Milwaukee, WI |
| www.thehymnsociety.org | The Hymn Society in the United States and Canada Book Service |
| www.musicanet.org | MUSICA, Strasbourg, France |
| www.ntimemusic.com | "N" Time Music, Charlotte, NC |
| www.ocp.org | Oregon Catholic Press, Portland, OR |

# African American Church Music Series Octavos
## GIA Publications, Inc.

**Amazing Grace** (NEW BRITAIN) Arr. Evelyn Simpson-Curenton SATB, Piano (7-E) G-5694 1.30

**Cast All Your Cares** Kevin Johnson SSA, Solo, Piano (7-E) G-5636 1.30

**Christ the Lord Is Risen Today** (EASTER HYMN) Arr. HOLLAND Includes stirring fanfare and interlude with modulation. SATB, Descant, Assembly, Organ, Brass Quartet, Timpani, Percussion (7-E) G-5850 1.30
Full Score and Parts G-5850-INST 22.00

**Done Made My Vow** Arr. Frederick B. Young SATB (5-E) G-5847 1.40

**Go Where I Send Thee** Arr. Uzee Brown, Jr. SATB (19-M) G-5777 1.70

**Go Where I Send Thee** Arr. Uzee Brown, Jr. TTBB (19-M) G-5778 1.60

**Good News, the Savior Is Born!** Glenn L. Jones SATB, Soprano Solo (7-E) G-5804 1.30

**Great Is Thy Faithfulness** William M. Runyan, arr. Nathan Carter SATB, Alto Solo, Piano (11-E/M) G-5590 1.50
Full orchestration available. Contact GIA for information.

**Guide My Feet** Arr. Avis D. Graves SATB, Piano (7-E) G-5952 1.30

**He Has the Power** from *The Mass of Saint Augustine* Leon C. Roberts SATB, Piano • (7-E/M) G-2476 1.30

**How Excellent Is Your Name** V. Michael McKay SATB, Piano (7-E) G-5848 1.40

**Hymn of Praise** Shelton Becton SATB, Acc. G-6027 In preparation

**I Want to See My Jesus Someday** Arr. Glen L. Jones Vocal Solo, Piano G-5805 In preparation

**I'm Willing, Lord** Kenneth W. Louis SATB, Solo, Piano • (7-E) G-6130 1.30

**If I Faint Not** Kevin & Celeste Johnson SATB, Solo, Piano (10-E/M) G-5635 1.40

**In the Beginning, God** Frank E. Williams SATB (7-E) G-5849 1.40

**It Is Well with My Soul** Phillip Bliss, arr. Nathan Carter SATB, Acc. (15-E/M) G-5868 1.50

**It Pays to Serve Jesus** Frank C. Huston, arr. Nathan Carter SATB, Tenor Solo, Piano (11-E) G-5875 1.40

**It's My Desire** Fred P. Bagley, Horace C. Boyer SATB, Piano (7-E) G-5589 1.30

**Jesus, You Brought Me All the Way** Kenneth W. Louis SATB, Solo, Piano • (7-E/M) G-6131 1.30

**Lazarus** Robert Tanner SATB, Tenor Solo (7-E) G-5851 1.40

**Lord, I Want to Live for Thee** Arr. Leo H. David, Jr. SATB, Solo, Organ (6 E) G-5806 1.30

**Lord, Make Me an Instrument** M. Roger Holland II SATB, Piano (11-E/M) G-5627 1.40
Full orchestration available. Contact GIA for information.

**More Love to Thee** Arr. Joseph Joubert *Medley of "More Love to Thee," "O How I Love Jesus," "My Jesus, I Love Thee," "Is There Anybody Here," and "My Soul Loves Jesus."* SATB, Soprano Solo, Piano (14-E/M) G-5843 1.50

**My God Is So High** Arr. Courtney Carey SSAATTBB (7-M) G-5896 1.30

**My Soul Is Anchored in the Lord** Arr. Charles Garner SATB, Tenor Solo, Piano (15-E) G-6137 1.60

**Nobody Knows the Trouble I See** Fernando G. Allen SATB (6-E) G-5830 1.30

**O for a Faith** Greatorex Collect, arr. Nathan Carter SATB, Contralto or Bass Solo, Acc. (7-E) G-5924 1.30

**O Worship the King** (LYONS) Johann J. Haydn, arr. Wendell C. Woods *In calypso style.* SATB, Piano (11-E) G-5810 1.40

**Precious Blood of Jesus, The** (Blood Medley) Arr. Jospeh Joubert SATB, Solo, Piano (14-M) G-5631 1.60

**Psalm 1** Nathan Carter SSATB, Acc. (10-E) G-6024 1.50

**Psalm 100** Verolga Nix SATB, Piano G-5829 In prepartion

**Psalm 121** Verolga Nix SATB, Piano G-5828 In preparation

**Psalm 150** Nathan Carter SATB, Soprano Solo, Organ (15-E) G-5591 1.50
Full orchestration available. Contact GIA for information.

**Rock-a My Soul** Arr. Uzee Brown, Jr. SSAATTBB with Soprano, Alto, and Bass Solos (7-M) G-5749 1.30

**Sanctify Me** V. Michael McKay SATB, Piano (5-E) G-5592 1.30

**Seek the Lord** Arr. Glenn L. Jones SATB, Soprano Solo (7-E) G-6025 1.40

**Shout for Joy (with Amen)** Dello Thedford SATB, Piano G-5846 In preparation

**Sing to the Lord a New Song** Willis L. Barnett SATB, Acc. G-5809 In preparation

**Sing to the Lord** Melvin E. Bryant, Jr. SATB (SSAATTBB), Piano (6-E/M) G-5593 1.30

**Some Day** C. A. Tindley, arr. Nathan Carter SSAATTBB, Solo, Organ (15-M) G-6023 1.60

**Song of Thanksgiving** Ronald L. Stevens, Sr. SATB, Piano (5-E) G-6057 1.40

**Speak to My Heart** J. E.ric Brown SATB, Soprano Solo, Piano (5-E/M) G-5594 1.30

**Stand by Me** C. A. Tindley, arr. Jewel T. Thompson SATB, Sopr. and Bar. Soli, Piano (9-E) G-5803 1.40

**Stop By, Lord** Doris W. Bettis SATB, Piano (5-E) G-5595 1.30

**Stop By, Lord: 14 Selections from the African American Church Music Series** Ed. ABBINGTON Collection • G-5974 29.00
*Includes recording CD-540 and one each of the following octavos:*
Stop By, Lord BETTIS - Sing to the Lord BRYANT - Nobody Knows the Trouble I See ALLEN - O for a Faith CARTER - Good News, the Savior Is Born! JONES - Stand by Me THOMPSON - Lord, make Me an Instrument HOLLAND - Rock-a My Soul U. BROWN - More Love to Thee JOUBERT - The Lord Will Hear the Just (with Proclaim God's Marvelous Deeds) LOUIS - It's My Desire BAGLEY, BOYER - Speak to My heart J. E. BROWN - Taste and See LOUIS - Sanctify Me McKAY

**Taste and See** from *Mass of St. Cyprian* Kennith W. Louis SATB, Piano (6-E/M) G-5637 1.30

**The Church's One Foundation** (AURELIA) Samuel S. Wesley, arr. M. Roger Holland II SATB, Organ, Opt. Brass Quartet, Timp, Percussion (10-E) G-5628 1.40
Full Score G-5628-FS 6.00
Full Score and Parts G-5628-INST 22.00

**The Lord Will Hear the Just / Proclaim God's Marvelous Deeds** Kennith W. Louis SATB, Acc (7-E) G-5744 1.30

**The Lord's Prayer** Charles Garner SATB, Piano (7-E) G-6026 1.40

**Three Spirituals** Arr. Joseph Joubert SATB (8-E) G-5925 1.50
Give Me Your Hand - In That Mornin' - Rockin' Jerusalem

**Wait for the Lord** Willis L. Barnett SATB, Acc. G-5808 In preparation

**We Are Climbing Jacob's Ladder** Horace C. Boyer SATB, Piano (5-E) G-5826 1.40

**What 'Cha Gonna Call the Pretty Little Baby** Arr. Ronald L. Stevens, Sr. SATB (3-E) G-6058 1.20

**Worthy Is the Lamb** Lamont Lenox SATB, Descant, Piano (7-E) G-5807 1.30

# Selected Bibliography

Abbington, James. *Let Mt. Zion Rejoice! Music in the African American Church.* Valley Forge, PA: Judson Press, 2001.

Abbington, James, editor. *Readings in African American Church Music and Worship.* Chicago: GIA Publications, Inc., 2001.

Abbington, James and Linda H. Hollies. *Waiting to Go! African American Church Worship Resources from Advent through Pentecost.* Chicago: GIA Publications, Inc., 2002.

Aghahowa, Brenda Eatman. *Praising in Black and White: Unity and Diversity in Christian* Worship. Cleveland: United Church Press, 1996.

Bell, Derrick. *Gospel Choirs: Psalms of Survival in an Alien Land Called Home.* New York: Basic Books, 1996.

Bell, John L. *The Singing Thing: A Case for Congregational Song.* Chicago: GIA Publications, 2000.

Bell. John L. *States of Bliss and Yearning: The Marks and Means of Authentic Christian Spirituality.* Chicago: GIA Publications, Inc., 2002.

Berglund, Brad. *Reinventing Sunday: Breakthrough Ideas for Transforming Worship.* Valley Forge, PA· Judson Press, 2001.

Berkley, James D., editor. *Leadership Handbook of Preaching and Worship.* Grand Rapids, MI: Baker Book House Co., 1992.

Black, Kathy. *Culturally Conscious Worship.* St. Louis, MO: Chalice Press, 2000.

Black, Kathy. *Worship Across Cultures: A Handbook.* Nashville: Abingdon Press, 1998.

Borsch, Frederick Houk. *Introducing the Lessons of the Church Year: A Guide for Lay Readers and Congregations.* New York: Seabury Press, 1978.

Bower, Peter C., editor. *Handbook for the Revised Common Lectionary.* Louisville, KY: Westminster John Knox Press, 1996.

Boyer, Horace Clarence. *How Sweet the Sound: The Golden Age of Gospel.* Washington, DC: Elliott and Clark Publishing, 1995.

Brink, Emily, ed. *Authentic Worship in a Changing Culture.* Grand Rapids, MI: CRC Publications, 1997.

Causey, C. Harry. *Things They Didn't Tell Me About Being A Minister of Music.* Rockville, MD: Music Revelation, 1988.

Chapman, Mark L. *Christianity on Trial: African-American Religious Thought Before and After Black Power.* Maryknoll, NY: Orbis Books, 1996.

Cherwien, David M. *Let the People Sing!* St. Louis: Concordia Publishing House, 1997.

Clark, Linda J., Joanne Swenson and Mark Stamm. *How We Seek God Together: Exploring Worship Style.* Bethesda, MD: The Alban Institute, 2002.

Cone, James H. *The Spiritual and the Blues.* Maryknoll, NY: Orbis Books, 1972.

Costen, Melva Wilson. *African American Christian Worship*. Nashville: Abingdon Press, 1993.

Davies, J. G., editor. *The New Westminster Dictionary of Liturgy and Worship*. Philadelphia: The Westminster Press, 1986.

Dawn, Marva J. *A Royal "Waste" of Time: The Splendor of Worshiping God and Being Church for the World*. Grand Rapids, MI: William B. Eerdmans Publishing Company, 1999.

Dawn, Marva J. *Reaching Out Without Dumbing Down: A Theology of Worship for the Turn of-the-Century Culture*. Grand Rapids, MI: William. B. Eerdmans Publishing Company, 1995.

DuBois, W.E.B. *The Souls of Black Folk*. New York: Dover Publications, 1994.

Dudley, Grenae D. and Carlyle F. Stewart III. *Sanfoka: Celebrations for the African-American Church*. Cleveland: United Church Press, 1997.

Dyson, Michael Eric. *Between God and Gangsta Rap: Bearing Witness to Black Culture*. New York: Oxford University Press, 1996.

Evans, Jr., James H. *We Have Been Believers: An African-American Systematic Theology*. Minneapolis: Fortress, 1992.

Evans, Jr., James H. *We Shall All Be Changed: Social Problems and Theological Renewal*. Minneapolis: Fortress, 1997.

Fisher, Miles Mark. *Negro Slave Songs in the United States*. New York: Citadel Press, 1953.

Floyd, Jr. Samuel A. *The Power of Black Music: Interpreting Its History from Africa to the United States*. New York: Oxford University Press, 1995.

Frame, John M. *Worship in Spirit and Truth: A Refreshing Study of the Principles and Practice of Biblical Worship*. Phillipsburg: P & R Publishing, 1996.

Franklin, Robert M. *Another Day's Journey: Black Churches Confronting the American Crisis*. Minneapolis: Fortress Press, 1997.

Goatley, David Emmanuel. *Were You There? Godforsakenness in Slave Religion*. Maryknoll, NY: Orbis Books, 1996.

Guimont, Michel. *Psalms for the Revised Common Lectionary*. Chicago: GIA Publications, Inc., 2000.

Harris, Michael W. *The Rise of Gospel Blues: The Music of Thomas Andrew* Dorsey *in the Urban Church*. New York: Oxford University Press, 1992.

Haas, David. *With Every Note I Sing: Prayers for Music Ministers and Those Who Love to Sing*. Chicago: GIA Publications, Inc., 1995.

Haas, David. *I Will Sing Forever: More Prayers for Music Ministers and Those Who Love to Sing*. Chicago: GIA Publications, Inc., 2001.

Hawn, C. Michael. *One Bread, One Body: Exploring Cultural Diversity in Worship*. Bethesda, MD: The Alban Institute, 2003.

Hayes, Diana L. *Were You There? Stations of the Cross*. Maryknoll, NY: Orbis Books, 2000.

Hickman, Hoyt L., Don E. Saliers, Laurence Hull Stokey, and James White. *The New Handbook of the Christian Year.* Nashville: Abingdon Press, 1992.

Holck, Jr., Manfred, compiler. *Dedication Services for Every Occasion.* Valley Forge, PA: Judson Press, 1984.

Holmes, Jr. Zan W. *Encountering Jesus.* Nashville: Abingdon Press, 1992.

Hollies, Linda H. *Trumpet in Zion: Worship Resources, Year A.* Cleveland: Pilgrim Press, 2001.

Hollies, Linda H. *Trumpet in Zion: Worship Resources, Year B.* Cleveland: The Pilgrim Press, 2002.

Hollies, Linda H. *Trumpet in Zion: Worship Resources, Year C.* Cleveland: The Pilgrim Press, 2003.

Hood, Robert E. *Begrimed and Black: Christian Traditions on Blacks and Blackness.* Minneapolis: Fortress Press, 1994.

Hood, Robert E. *Must God Remain Greek? Afro Cultures and God-talk.* Minneapolis: Fortress Press, 1990.

Hurston, Zola Neale. *The Sanctified Church.* Berkeley, CA: Turtle Island, 1981.

Jackson, Irene V., editor. *Afro-American Religious Music: A Bibliography and Catalogue of Gospel Music* Westport, NY: Greenwood Press, 1979.

Jones, Arthur C. *Wade in the Water: The Wisdom on the Spirituals.* Maryknoll, NY: Orbis Books, 1993.

Jones, Kirk Byron. *Rest in the Storm: Self Care Strategies for Clergy and Other Caregivers.* Valley Forge, PA: Judson Press, 2001.

Jordan, James. *The Musician's Soul.* Chicago: GIA Publications, 1999.

Jordan, James. *The Musician's Spirit: Connecting to Others Through Story.* Chicago: GIA Publicatons, Inc. 2002.

Keener, Craig S. and Glenn Usry. *Defending Black Faith: Answers to Tough Questions about African-American Christianity.* Downers Grove, IL: Inter-Varsity Press, 1997.

Keikert, Patrick R. *Welcoming the Stranger: A Public Theology of Worship and Evangelism.* Minneapolis: Fortress Press, 1992.

Kirk-Duggan, Cheryl A. *African American Special Days: 15 Complete Worship Services.* Nashville: Abingdon Press, 1996.

Kirk-Duggan, Cheryl A. *Exorcizing Evil: A Womanist Perspective on the Spirituals.* Maryknoll, NY: Orbis Books, 1997.

Laster, James. *Catalogue of Choral Music Arranged in Biblical Order.* Second Edition. Lanham, MD: Scarecrow Press, 1996.

Lehman, Victor. *The Pastor's Guide to Weddings and Funerals.* Valley Forge, PA: Judson Press, 2001.

Liesch, Barry. *The New Worship: Straight Talk on Music and the Church.* Grand Rapids, MI: Baker Book House Co., 1996.

Lincoln, C. Eric and Lawrence Mamiya. *The Black Church in the African American Experience.* Durham, NC: Duke University Press, 1990.

Long, Thomas G. *Beyond the Worship Wars: Building Vital and Faithful Worship.* Bethesda, MD: The Alban Institute, 2001.

Lovell, Jr., John. *Black Song: The Forge and the Flame.* New York: Macmillan, 1972.

Mapson, Jr., J. Wendell. *The Ministry of Music in the Black Church.* Valley Forge, PA: Judson Press. 1984.

Mapson, Jr., J. Wendell. *Strange Fire: A Study of Worship and Liturgy in the African American Church.* St. Louis: Hodale Press, 1996.

McClain. William B. *Come Sunday: The Liturgy of Zion.* Nashville: Abingdon Press, 1990.

Webb-Mitchell, Brett and Diane Archer. *Sacred Seasons: A Journey Through the Church Year.* Cleveland: The Pilgrim Press, 2002.

Mitchell, Robert H. *I Don't Like That Music.* Carol Steam, IL: Hope Publishing Company, 1993.

Moffett, Diane Givens. *Beyond Greens and Cornbread: Reflections on African American Christian Identity.* Valley Forge, PA: Judson Press, 2002.

Moleck, Fred and Robert Oldershaw. *Scripture Reflections for the Church Musician.* Chicago: GIA Publications, Inc., 1993.

Orr, N. Lee. *The Church Music Handbook for Pastors and Musicians.* Nashville: Abingdon Press, 1991.

Owens, Bill. *The Magnetic Music Ministry.* Nashville: Abingdon Press, 1996.

Pitts Jr., Walter F. *Old Ship of Zion: The Afro-Baptist Ritual in the African Diaspora.* New York: Oxford University Press, 1993.

Raboteau, Albert J. *Slave Religion: The "Invisible Institution" in the Antebellum South.* New York: Oxford University Press, 1978.

Raboteau, Robert J. *A Fire in the Bones: Reflections on African-American Religious History.* Boston: Beacon Press, 1995.

Reagon, Bernice Johnson, editor. *We'll Understand It Better By and By: Pioneering African-American Gospel Composers.* Washington, DC: Smithsonian Institution Press, 1992.

Ross, Andrew and Tricia Rose, editors. *Microphones Fiends: Youth Music and Youth Culture.* New York: Routledge, 1994.

Sanders, Cheryl J. *Saints in Exile: The Holiness-Pentecostal Experience in African American Religion and Culture.* New York: Oxford University Press, 1996.

Southern, Eileen. *Readings in Black American Music.* New York: W. W. Norton and Company, 1971.

Southern, Eileen. *The Music of Black Americans: A History.* Third Edition. New York: W. W. Norton and Company, 1997.

Spencer, Donald A. *Hymn and Scripture Selection Guide: A Cross-Reference Tool for Worship Leaders.* Grand Rapids, MI: Baker Book House, 1993.

Spencer, Jon Michael. *Black Hymnody: A Hymnological History of the African-American Church.* Knoxville, TN: The University of Tennessee Press, 1992.

Spencer, Jon Michael. *Protest and Praise: Sacred Music of Black Religion.* Minneapolis: Fortress Press, 1990.

Spencer, Jon Michael. *Sing a New Song: Liberating Black Hymnody.* Minneapolis: Fortress Press, 1995.

Stewart III, Carlyle F. *Black Spirituality and Black Consciousness: Soul Force, Culture and Freedom in the African-American Experience.* Trenton, NJ: Africa World Press, 1999.

Stewart III, Carlyle F. *Soul Survivors: An African American Spirituality.* Louisville: Westminster John Knox Press, 1997.

Stewart III, Carlyle F. *African American Church Growth: 12 Principles for Prophetic Ministry.* Nashville: Abingdon Press, 1994.

Talbot, Frederick H. *African American Worship: New Eyes for Seeing.* Lima, OH: Fairway Press, 1998.

Turner, Steve. *Amazing Grace: The Story of America's Most Beloved Song.* New York: Ecco - A Division of HarperCollins Publishers, 2002.

*The Revised Common Lectionary: The Consultation on Common Texts.* Nashville: Abingdon Press, 1992.

Walker, Wyatt Tee. *Somebody's Calling My Name: Black Sacred Music and Social Change.* Valley Forge, PA: Judson Press, 1979.

Walker, Wyatt Tee. *Spirits that Dwell in Deep Woods: The Prayer and Praise Hymns of the Black Religious Experience,* edited by James Abbington. Chicago; GIA Publications, 2003.

Warren, Gwendolin Sims. *Ev'ry Time I Feel the Spirit: 101 Best-Loved Psalms, Gospel Hymns, and Spiritual Songs of the African-American Church.* New York: Henry Holt and Company, 1997.

Washington, James Melvin. *Conversations With God. Two Centuries of Prayers by African Americans.* New York: HarperCollins Publishers, 1994.

Webber, Robert E. *Worship is a Verb: Eight Principles for Transforming Worship.* Second Edition. Peabody, MA: Hendrickson Publishers, 1995.

Webber, Robert. *Planning Blended Worship: The Creative Mixture of Old and New.* Nashville: Abingdon Press, 1998.

Westermeyer, Paul. *Let Justice Sing: Hymnody and Justice.* Collegeville, MN: The Liturgical Press, 1998.

Westermeyer, Paul. *Te Deum: The Church and Music.* Minneapolis: Fortress, 1998.

Westermeyer, Paul. *With Tongues of Fire: Profiles in 20th-Century Hymn Writing.* St. Louis: Concordia Publishing House, 1995.

Wilmore, Gayraud S. *Last Things First: Library of Living Faith.* Philadelphia: The Westminster Press, 1982,

Wimbush, Vincent L., editor. *African Americans and The Bible: Sacred Texts and Social Textures.* New York: Continuum International Publishing Group, 2000.

Wren, Brian. *Praying Twice: The Music and Words of Congregational Song.* Louisville, KY: Westminster John Knox Press, 2000.

Wright, Jr. Jeremiah A. *Africans Who Shaped the Faith: A Study of 10 Biblical Personalities.* Chicago: Urban Ministries, 1995.